Dinner Parties

RECIPES

Georgeanne Brennan

GENERAL EDITOR

Chuck Williams

PHOTOGRAPHY

Keller & Keller

FOOD STYLING

Alison Attenborough

STYLING

Lauren Hunter

TEXT

Steve Siegelman

BONNIER
BOOKS

CONTENTS

REDISCOVERING THE DINNER PARTY

There are dinners, and then there are dinner parties. Dinners are about sharing good food with others. But dinner parties are something more than simply meals. After all, they are parties, and what distinguishes a party from a meal is a sense of style and a vision that defines everything from the guest list and seating plan to the food, drinks and decor. A dinner party—whether formal or casual—is a work of art, a harmonious whole, a special occasion.

Of course, all of us are pressed for time these days. But that doesn't mean we need to sacrifice the pleasures of the table and entertaining. Indeed, nowadays, a gracious dinner party is more appreciated than ever. And even though life seems to grow more hectic with every passing day, it is good to remember that with a little organisation, strategic shopping and a plan for getting most of the work done in advance, you can host a dinner party with a minimum of stress.

This book was designed with that kind of thinking in mind. The party menus, recipes, style ideas and planning tips were created for people who love food and entertaining but don't have a lot of time. The secret to it all: keeping things simple and adding imaginative touches that turn a gathering into a celebration, whether it is an elegant sit-down dinner or a casual supper on the patio.

In each chapter, you'll find everything you need to create a complete party. But you can also choose recipes and ideas from anywhere in the book to plan an event that works best for your occasion and your space. You don't need fancy china or special skills to be a great host. All it takes to master the art of hosting a dinner party are straightforward, company-friendly recipes, a few inventive ideas, an organised approach and your own unique sense of style.

DINNER PARTY PLANNING

The key to a successful dinner party is to stay organised by breaking down the work of planning, shopping and cooking into manageable, do-ahead tasks. In these pages, you'll find menus, serving strategies and decorating ideas for gatherings both small and large, casual and elegant. Use them as a starting point and you'll master the skills to hosting a dinner party with confidence and ease.

The Occasion

Begin by choosing a theme that will tie the entire party together. Take your cue from the occasion (a birthday, anniversary, holiday or major milestone), the season, and your guest list. It might be an elegant soirée, a cosy midwinter supper by the hearth or an informal outdoor gathering.

When and Where

Next, choose a day and a location that will fit your desired theme. Look for creative ways to use your space that make the most of its best features, perhaps staging your party in the kitchen, family room or on the patio. A 7:00 pm starting time works well for most dinners. Allow an hour for cocktails and mingling before the meal.

Guest List and Invitations

Jot down a list of guests to invite and round it out by adding people with complementary interests and backgrounds. Add a few extra names in case you need to invite more people. If you are including children, invite enough to make up a group.

For casual get-togethers, an e-mailed invitation or a phone call is appropriate.

More formal parties call for invitations sent through the mail. Don't forget to include all the details, including RSVP information. Allow four to six weeks' advance notice for formal occasions, less for informal ones.

Dinner Party Style

As you plan your party, stand in the middle of the space and think about how it will come together. Do you envision an informal gathering or a dressy sit-down dinner? Will the food be served family style, buffet style or as a series of plated courses? Does the party call for special decorations and place cards or just a few flowers and candles?

Whatever style you choose, give some thought to the pre-dinner phase of the evening. Plan to greet guests with cocktails, wine or sparkling wine and a non-alcoholic option. Along with drinks, offer an appetiser or two. For more formal events, consider a tray of hors d'oeuvre; for casual dinners, set out nuts, olives and other salty snacks.

Planning the Menu

Once you've settled on the theme, setting and style of your dinner party, you can begin thinking about the food and drinks. Use the menus in this book for inspiration, mixing and matching as needed to fit your occasion and suit your taste. If possible, try out each recipe ahead of time to get a sense of timing, flavour and presentation.

Seasonality and Balance

As any chef will tell you, seasonality is the most important guideline in planning a menu. In-season ingredients offer the best flavour and often the best prices. Think about dishes that match the weather, too: a grilled entrée with room-temperature vegetables on a warm summer evening, a hearty braised dish with polenta on an autumn or winter night.

Consider the menu as a whole and choose complementary and contrasting colours, textures, tastes and serving temperatures. Balance a rich starter with a light main course, or a chilled soup or appetiser salad with a more substantial main course. Keep individual flavours focused and simple, so each element of the meal has its own distinctive character.

Be Realistic

Give some thought to the realities of your kitchen, your skill level, your budget and your schedule. The larger the group, the less complicated your menu should be. Choose dishes that can be made in advance (you'll want to prepare as much as possible before guests arrive), and don't hesitate to use some high-quality shop-bought ingredients, such as spreads and sauces, antipasti from a specialty deli, premium ice cream or a dessert from a favourite local bakery.

Planning the Drinks

Begin with the basics: red and white wine or rosé; still and sparkling water; and, for casual meals, beer. You may want to start the evening with a signature cocktail along with a non-alcoholic option. Don't forget to plan for coffee (offer regular and decaf), tea and after-dinner drinks, such as dessert wine, brandy, port or liqueurs.

Displaying the Menu

For large dinner parties and special occasions, individual menus give guests an idea of what's ahead. Choose attractive paper, and write out menus by hand or print them on the computer. Set them on or beside each place setting, or display a single menu as part of the table decor.

Transforming the Space

Adding a few simple style touches will make your party more special and your guests more comfortable. Begin by removing clutter and excess furniture and then cleaning. Now you are ready to start transforming your space.

Lighting

First, turn off or dim overhead lights. Place scent-free, dripless candles on the table, on food and drink stations, and in conversation areas to create a feeling of warmth. At the dinner table, use low candles (votives or pillars) or tall (tapers in candelabras) so sight lines are not blocked. For outdoor parties, use strings of lanterns to contain the space and add sparkle.

Music

Assemble a playlist ahead of time, choosing selections that fit the party's theme, or set aside CDs. Keep the volume at a level that allows everyone to converse easily.

Seating

A seating plan ensures a lively mix at the table. Set out place cards, or simply direct guests to their seats. Your chairs don't need to match, as long as they are comfortable; add cushions if necessary. Slipcovers or a decorative element tied to each chair back will help create a uniform look.

Making the Most of the Room

Rearrange furniture to create areas where guests can gather in small groups before and after the meal. Allow plenty of space between furniture for smooth traffic flow.

BEVERAGE PLANNING

Bottled Water Chill 1 large bottle for every 2 guests; have both sparkling and still on hand.

Wine or Sparkling Wine Have on hand 1 bottle for every 2 or 3 wine drinkers, plus a few extra bottles.

Beer Plan on 2 to 3 bottles for every beer drinker; offer at least two different types, light and dark.

Spirits Buy 1 litre for every 10 to 12 drinkers.

Coffee For drip coffee, calculate 1 heaped tablespoon of freshly ground coffee per cup (250 g (8 oz) yields about 25 cups).

Tea Have several varieties of tea for guests to choose from. A refreshing Earl Grey or delicate herb or fruit tea adds variety. These all come in bags.

Ice Plan on 500-750 g (1-1½ lb) of ice per person, or more if chilling wine and bottled drinks. (If making your own ice, use filtered or bottled water to avoid off flavours).

THE PARTY PANTRY

Keep a supply of salty snacks and party foods on hand for impromptu entertaining.

- Jars of olives and marinated vegetables
- Crackers, flat breads, potato crisps, and bread sticks
- Tortilla chips and salsa
- Tapenade, artichoke spread, sun-dried tomato spread and truffle paste
- Almonds, cashews, peanuts, pistachios and spiced walnuts

SERVING EQUIPMENT

Outfitting your home with a few essential items will make any dinner party easier.

- Platters, trays and boards for serving
- Salad bowl
- Bread basket and butter crocks
- Small dishes for olives, nuts and dips
- Salt and pepper cellars, shakers or mills
- Cheese board, knives and spreaders
- Wine cooler, ice bucket, corkscrew, jugs, coasters and cocktail napkins

Serving Styles

As your menu takes shape, think about the best way to serve the food, taking into account the number of guests, the level of formality, the complexity of the menu and the realities of your space. You can mix styles, too, such as plating the first course and serving the rest family style.

Restaurant Style

For more formal parties, plating individual plates in the kitchen or by the host at the head of the table is a good option. This allows you to compose and garnish each plate and works well if your table is too small to hold many serving platters.

Buffet Style

A self-service buffet with food set at one or more tables works for formal and informal parties, especially for larger groups. You can use the dining table for the buffet and invite guests to eat in other rooms.

Family Style

Passing food on platters at the table is ideal for an informal party. Let guests pass smaller side dishes while you circulate with the main course and serve each guest. If your table is small, set the platters on a side table after everyone is served.

Outdoor

Outdoor meals tend to be casual and call for simplicity, making family-style or buffet service good choices. Include some cold dishes to make serving easier and position the dining table to allow easy access to the kitchen. Have ready clothespegs to secure the tablecloth, hurricane lamps to shield candles and alternative seating plans in case the weather changes.

Staying Organised

Have all the details under control when your guests arrive—the space set for entertaining, the food and drinks ready to serve, the kitchen clean—and you will be able to relax and enjoy your party.

Make Lists

Start a to-do list and a shopping list as soon as you begin planning your party. Organise the to-do list in chronological order and the shopping list by categories (produce, meat, and so on) for efficient shopping. Write down both the menu and a timetable for cooking and serving.

Shop Strategically

Finish most of your shopping a day or two before the party, leaving only a few items to the last minute. Save time by calling ahead to reserve major purchases, such as meat, fish and wine, so your order is ready to pick up. Ask for items to be as fully prepared as possible: meats and fish boned, oysters shucked, crab cracked.

Clean As You Go

Allow plenty of advance time to clean the house, including stocking the bathroom with fresh towels and soap. Wash pots and pans as you cook so the kitchen is clean when the party starts. Organise your refrigerator for easy access, and then just before the guests arrive, give the kitchen floor a quick sweep.

Selecting Wine

Serving a variety of wines at a single meal can make the dinner more special. Wines are often better appreciated when they progress from white to red and lighter to heavier over the course of the evening.

Sparkling wines, which include French Champagne, Italian Prosecco, Spanish *cava* and California bottlings, pair nicely with hors d'oeuvres and can be served with a first course or with dessert.

White wines range from light-bodied (Riesling, Pinot Gris, Soave) to medium-bodied (Bordeaux, Sauvignon Blanc) to full-bodied (Chardonnay). They vary in sweetness, with a crisp, dry Chardonnay or Bordeaux at one end of the spectrum and a fruitier Riesling or Gewürztraminer at the other. Likewise, red wines also range from light-bodied (Bardolino, Beaujolais) to medium-bodied (Merlot, Pinot Noir) to full-bodied (Cabernet Sauvignon, Syrah).

Dessert wines, such as Sauternes, Tokay, and *vin santo,* are smooth, rich and sweet, while fortified wines (Madeira, port, sherry) are ideal aperitifs or digestifs.

How to Chill and Serve Wine

Serve sparkling wines very cold (6°–7°C /42°–45°F), whites cold (10°C/50°F), and reds at cool room temperature. White wines should be chilled for at least 2 hours in the refrigerator or at least 20 minutes in an ice bucket (equal parts ice and water).

If serving more than one wine at dinner, include appropriate glasses for each wine at every place setting. Pour wine once the guests are seated, filling only to the widest part of the bowl, so the wine can be swirled to bring out its flavour and aroma. Aim the wine into the centre of the bowl, and then lightly twist the bottle so the last drop falls into the glass. Pour sparkling wine down the side of the glass, starting with a small amount, letting the foam settle, and then filling the glass about three-quarters full.

Wrap chilled bottles in a cloth napkin before serving to insulate and prevent drips. Decanters or carafes help mellow out very young or tannic wines and can also add a decorative accent to the table.

MATCHING FOOD AND WINE

Set aside rules like "red with meat, white with fish." Think about the characteristics of the dish (light, rich, etc.) and choose wines that mirror or contrast those qualities.

TYPE OF FOOD	WINE MATCH
Appetisers and savoury snacks	Sparkling wines: *Champagne, Prosecco, cava*
Spicy, salty or smoked dishes	Fruity, light-bodied wines: *Riesling, Gewürztraminer, Gruner Veltliner, rosé, Pinot Gris, Lambrusco, Pinot Noir*
Acidic dishes	High-acid wines: *white Bordeaux, Sauvignon Blanc, Zinfandel, Chianti*
Braised, roasted or grilled beef	Full-bodied reds: *Cabernet Sauvignon, Barbaresco, Barolo, Zinfandel, Rioja, Sangiovese, Syrah*
Roasted or grilled chicken and fish	Dry whites: *Albariño, Chardonnay, Pinot Grigio, Sancerre, Vermentino, Viognier*
Roasted or grilled lamb	Medium-bodied reds: *Burgundy, Côtes du Rhône, Merlot, Pinot Noir, Tempranillo*
Desserts	Sweet wines: *Sauternes, vin santo, Muscat, port*

Centrepieces

A centrepiece serves as the focal point for the table and helps transform the room. Creating an attractive one is surprisingly easy. The trick is to keep it understated and natural, such as an informal seasonal arrangement of fresh flowers, fruits, vegetables or plants. You'll want to make your centrepieces low or airy so they don't block sight lines across the table.

Flowers

Visit a flower market or florist to buy blooms and greenery a day or two before the party. If using flowers from your garden, snip them in the early morning or late evening, cutting their stems on the diagonal with pruning shears, and place them in cool water until you're ready to arrange them.

Choose flowers in a single colour and then add just one or two complementary shades. Make sure their fragrance isn't too strong or it might conflict with the aromas of the foods. Remember, too, a large quantity of a single kind of bloom can often deliver a more vivid impression than a few higher-priced flowers or a busy combination of different colors and shapes.

Herbs, Branches and Plants

Fresh herbs and branches can be used to round out floral arrangements or to make beautiful centrepieces on their own. Buy decorative foliage, such as curly willow, cherry, dogwood or grapevines, as well as flowering herbs, such as rosemary, thyme and lavender, or simply gather appealing branches and herbs from your garden. Arrange them in shallow vases or directly on the surface of the table for a casual look.

Potted herbs and plants, such as ivy, hydrangeas or miniature roses, also work well as table decorations. Choose low, nicely shaped plants, and repot them, if desired, in containers that fit your theme and decor. At the end of the meal, you can give them to guests as gifts to take home.

Fruits and Vegetables
Seasonal fruits, such as lemons and limes, miniature apples or pomegranates, or vegetables, such as artichokes, flowering cabbage or peppers, can make an attractive centrepiece. The more subtle and restrained the colour palette, the more elegant the result will be. Build your arrangement on a tray or footed platter, a low glass bowl or directly on the tabletop, adding complementary flowers or greenery if you like.

Making an Arrangement

Avoid the temptation to slip a store-bought bouquet into a vase "as is." In just a few minutes, you can create an arrangement that works perfectly for your table. When choosing a vase, be imaginative. Consider low, unobtrusive vases, bowls (for floating blossoms) or other types of containers, such as jars or jugs in clear glass or neutral tones or galvanized buckets. Set up a work area and gather shears, vases and something to anchor the flowers, if needed, such as floral foam, marbles, stones or a flower frog (a metal stand with sharp metal pins used to keep stems in place).

Stand the flowers you plan to use next to the vase to gauge how tall they should be and trim their stems on the diagonal, stripping away any leaves that would be submerged in the water. Arrange the blooms in a pleasing shape, such as a tight bundle, a cascading bouquet or even just a few loose stems. If using blooms of different heights, work from tallest to shortest, placing the tallest blooms in the centre. If necessary, use an anchoring device to hold the blooms in place, then add greenery or branches as needed to fill gaps. Add some flower food or a few drops of bleach to the water to extend the life of the arrangement. Change the water every two days, and recut the stems if browned.

Most flowers should be cut and arranged a day ahead of time so they are fully opened by the evening of the party. Buy extra flowers and greenery to decorate individual place settings, or to create smaller satellite arrangements, for placing on the buffet or mantel and in the entrance hall and bathroom to tie the whole space together. Have extra vases on hand in case guests bring flowers to the party.

SEASONAL FLOWERS AND BRANCHES

SEASON	FLOWERS
Spring	Apple and cherry blossoms, daffodils, dogwood, forsythia, irises, lilacs, lilies, narcissi, peonies, ranunculus, sweet peas, tulips, violets
Summer	Chrysanthemums, cornflowers, daisies, forget-me-nots, Gerber daisies, hydrangeas, lavender, roses, sunflowers
Autumn	Asters, bittersweet, chrysanthemums, cosmos, dahlias, gladioli, hyacinths, marigolds, olive branches, rosehips
Winter	Citrus, daffodils, greenery (holly, ivy and evergreen boughs), narcissi, persimmons, poinsettias, quinces
Year-round	Carnations, gardenias, hydrangeas, orchids, roses

Glassware

You don't need a large collection of matching glassware, but you do need pieces of similar quality that reflect your taste and style. Choose pieces that feel substantial in your hand. If you own crystal, don't store it away for special occasions. Its sparkle will enliven even the most casual table setting.

Wineglasses

Well-made wineglasses can enhance the experience of drinking wine. Look for glasses that are thin-walled and clear with a cut and polished rim. A basic collection should include tulip-shaped large red-wine glasses and smaller white-wine and dessert-wine glasses, though a standard 310-ml (10 oz) white-wine glass is acceptable to use for any kind of wine. Stemless wineglasses are easy to hold and have a contemporary look well suited to both formal and casual settings.

Flutes are used for serving Champagne and other sparkling wines. Their tall, tapered shape traps and preserves the bubbles and concentrates the aroma and effervescence of the wine.

Cocktail Glasses

Cocktail glasses with V-shaped bowls can be used for any mixed drink served without ice. Slightly larger martini glasses are used for martinis, cosmopolitans and blender drinks. A well-stocked glassware collection also includes old-fashioned glasses (small tumblers for mixed drinks and drinks served with ice) and highball or Collins glasses (taller, straight-sided glasses for mixed drinks and blender drinks).

Water Glasses

Virtually any glass with a capacity of at least 180 ml (6 oz) can be used as a water glass, but the most popular choices are small tumblers or for more formal settings, short, stemmed goblets.

Dinnerware

Don't be concerned about how fancy or formal your pieces are. The only rule is to choose items with a quiet sense of style that won't upstage the food.

Plates

Dinnerware falls into five categories, from casual to refined: pottery earthenware, stoneware, porcelain and bone china. Stay with one type throughout the meal, but feel free to mix and match pieces from different sets, especially for separate courses. For formal dinners, you will need a charger and dinner, salad, bread and dessert plates.

Bowls

Serve first-course soups, pastas and risottos in shallow soup bowls. Deep bowls are fine for serving hearty pastas, soups and stews at casual dinners. Both shallow and deep bowls can be used for unstructured desserts, such as fruit crumbles or ice cream.

Cutlery

A basic place setting includes a standard fork, a salad and/or dessert fork, a knife, a teaspoon and a soup spoon, sometimes augmented with a butter knife and a steak knife. Stainless steel is a good choice for most dinner parties, with sterling silver or silver plate usually reserved for special occasions since it has to be washed by hand and polished. Look for sturdy pieces with a timeless, classic design.

Serving dishes

Choose versatile serving pieces that will fit any style or occasion, such as white platters and bowls and silver or stainless-steel utensils, then branch out to include coloured or patterned pieces in your collection.

Platters

You'll need at least two platters, one oval and one rectangular, for serving main courses and finger-food appetisers. Footed platters are traditional for cakes and pies, but can also be used for appetisers, fruit and cheese. Two or three smaller platters are handy for side dishes and appetisers.

Other Serving Vessels

A well-rounded collection includes a few large bowls for potatoes, polenta and the like; a salad bowl; a soup tureen; and small bowls for nuts, olives and other appetisers. A large, shallow bowl is useful for pastas, vegetable side dishes and fruit salads. Supplement your collection with large jugs and decanters or carafes for water, wine and other drinks; a gravy boat; and small jugs for syrups, sauces and cream.

Utensils

A few key serving utensils are all you need: all-purpose spoons, salad servers, tongs, a ladle, a serving fork for meat and poultry, a pasta fork, a spatula for fish and baked dishes, a cheese knife and spreader and a dessert server for cake or tart.

GLASSWARE

Decanter | Red-wine glass | White-wine glass | Dessert-wine glass | Champagne flute | Stemless wineglass | Tumbler | Martini glass | Cocktail glass

DINNERWARE & SERVINGWARE

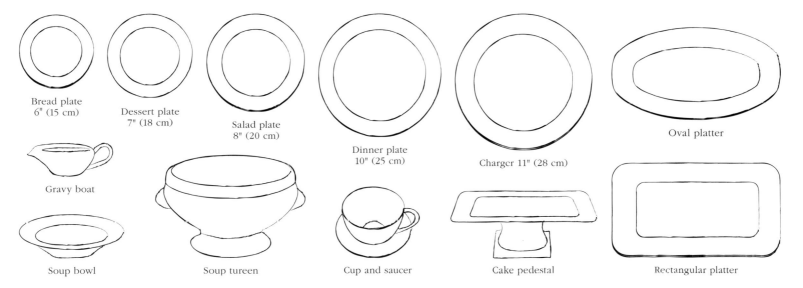

Bread plate 6" (15 cm)

Dessert plate 7" (18 cm)

Salad plate 8" (20 cm)

Dinner plate 10" (25 cm)

Charger 11" (28 cm)

Oval platter

Gravy boat

Soup bowl

Soup tureen

Cup and saucer

Cake pedestal

Rectangular platter

SERVING UTENSILS

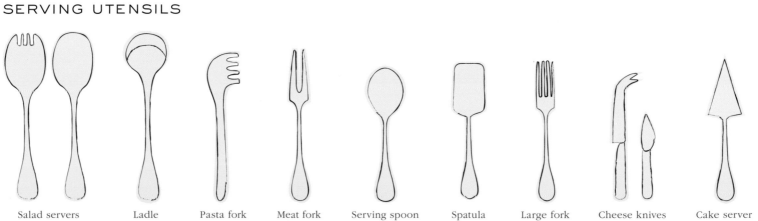

Salad servers | Ladle | Pasta fork | Meat fork | Serving spoon | Spatula | Large fork | Cheese knives | Cake server

Hosting a Formal Dinner

Formal entertaining should always be more about *special occasion* than *formality*. It should be fun and enjoyable for both the host and the guests—a chance to mark an event in a festive way, with good food, a welcoming table and the kind of small extravagances that make people happy.

Setting the Table

Formal table settings are steeped in tradition. But think of such customs only as guidelines to help create a gracious mood and comfortable table. Break out the good china and linens, and feel free to add your own creative touches.

THE FINE POINTS

When planning your party, take time to think through the finishing touches.

Salt and Pepper Set out salt and pepper dispensers for every two guests.

Bread and Butter Serve warm dinner rolls in a linen-lined basket. Portion butter into pats, curls, or balls or serve in ramekins.

Water Serve chilled still and sparkling water from glass carafes or jugs.

Wine Keep bottles or decanters on the table or sideboard; chill white wines in an ice bucket.

Coffee and Tea After the main course, set up coffee and tea service on the sideboard.

Cheese Before dessert, offer cheeses on a marble slab with nuts or dried fruit.

After-dinner Drinks Arrange drinks on a tray and serve at or away from the table.

Begin by creating a seating plan. The hosts traditionally sit at the head and foot of the table, with a female guest of honor sitting to the right of the male host and a male guest of honor to the right of the female host. Seat guests with common interests next to each other, alternating men and women, if possible and put a place card at each plate. The cards can be omitted for the hosts, and should be cleared after the first course.

Set the table with a tablecloth and matching napkins, allowing enough room between settings (about 60 cm/2 ft) from the centre of one plate to the next). Put a charger, or oversized service plate, as a placeholder at each setting, then clear it when the main course is served.

Next, lay the cutlery at each setting, putting the pieces used first farthest from the plate, so guests work inward as the meal progresses. Arrange all the glassware needed for the meal in a diagonal line above the knife in order of use from left to right, starting with the water glass. Set a butter plate and knife above the forks.

Serving the Meal

Platters of hors d'oeuvres can be set out or passed while guests enjoy cocktails in the living room or on the patio. When it is time to move to the table, light the candles and fill the water glasses. You can have the first course at each place before the guests sit down, or serve a passed or plated first course once they are seated.

The main course and side dishes can be individually plated in the kitchen and served restaurant style, but this approach can be time-consuming and takes you away from the table and guests. A good compromise is to have the main course and side dishes on platters at the head of the table, where you can compose the plates and pass them to the guests. Remove the platters to a sideboard until it is time to offer seconds, and then pass the platters. Make sure you stand to the left of guests so they can use their right hand to help themselves and that each platter is accompanied with an appropriate serving spoon and/or fork.

Dessert can be served in the same way: individually plated in the kitchen or served from the head of the table by the host. Coffee and tea can be poured in the kitchen or at the sideboard, with refills offered by the host at the table. Keep an eye on guests' water and wine and refill glasses as needed.

Clearing the Table

Clearing should be done unobtrusively by the hosts after each course, with the help of a previously recruited guest if the group is large. Wait until everyone has finished eating, then clear plates from the right, taking only two at a time to avoid stacking or juggling silverware. To save time, return from the kitchen with plates for the next course to replace those just cleared.

Before dessert, clear the dishes from the last course, along with unused cutlery, bread plates, salt and pepper cellars and wineglasses that are no longer being used. Using a folded napkin, brush crumbs from the table onto a small tray or plate. Reset the table with any other needed cutlery that will be used for dessert.

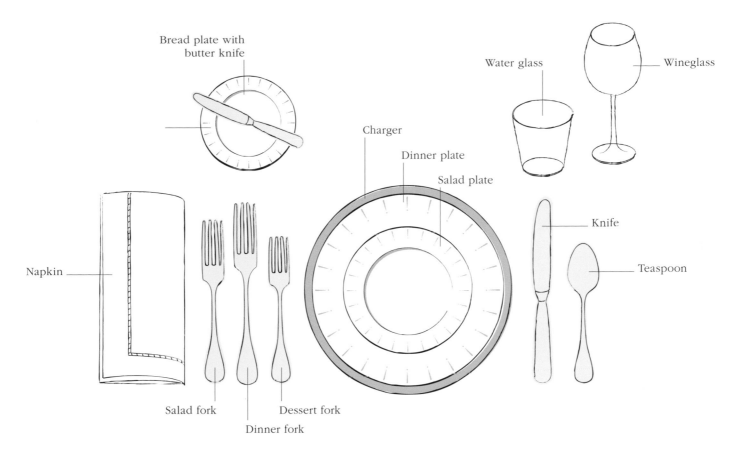

Bread plate with butter knife

Water glass

Wineglass

Charger

Dinner plate

Salad plate

Knife

Napkin

Teaspoon

Salad fork

Dessert fork

Dinner fork

FORMAL SETTING

Here are the essential elements for a formal setting, which will vary according to your menu, your personal preferences and the pieces you own.

Napkin A folded napkin is placed to the left of the forks, its folded side facing the plate, ready to be picked up and laid across the lap as a guest sits down. Or it is put on the centre of the plate, especially when folded in a creative way.

Bread Plate with Butter Knife Set a small plate for bread just above the forks, and lay a small butter knife across it so it faces the left on a slight diagonal.

Salad Fork Forks are placed to the left of the plate in order of use from left to right. If salad is to be served before the main course, set the salad fork in the outermost position; if after, place it to the right of the dinner fork. The salad fork can also be used for other first courses.

Dinner Fork The dinner fork, used for the main course, is the largest fork in the setting.

Dessert Fork Slightly smaller than the salad fork, the dessert fork is set nearest to the dinner plate at the start of the meal, or brought out with the dessert course. If you do not own dessert forks, wash and dry the salad forks for dessert.

Charger Also known as the service plate, the charger is used in the initial place setting and remains as a liner under the first-course plate until the main course is served.

Dinner Plate This large plate is used for the main course and side dishes. Warm, if possible, in a microwave or low oven just before serving.

Salad Plate This small plate can also be used for first courses and desserts. It is often chilled when used for serving salads or other first courses.

Knife A sturdy table knife is set to the right of the plate, its blade facing inward. If you are serving steaks, chops or roasted meat, you may use steak knives in place of table knives.

Teaspoon Place a teaspoon to the right of the knife. Or, you can bring out the teaspoons at the same time you bring out the coffee and tea. If serving soup, place a soup spoon to the right of the teaspoon.

Water Glass Set a tumbler or goblet for water just above the knife. Fill water glasses just before the guests are seated.

Wineglass To the right and slightly above the water glass, set the wineglass for the first wine being served (usually a white). For each additional wine you plan to pour, place another wineglass to the right of the previous one on a slight diagonal.

Even the most casual dinner parties can benefit from a few special serving touches.

Salt and Pepper Set out a few pairs of salt and pepper shakers, or use small dishes as cellars and garnish with herb sprigs.

Bread and Butter Serve warm bread in a linen-lined basket or on a small wooden cutting board, or put baguettes directly on the table. Pack butter, plain or flavoured with herbs, in small crocks.

Water and Wine Place bottles or carafes on the table or keep on the sideboard and refill glasses throughout the evening.

Coffee and Tea Place freshly brewed pots on the table or serve from the sideboard.

DINNER PARTY TIPS

- Pick a colour palette and use it for everything, from invitations to place cards to decorative accents.

- Try out recipes at least once before putting them on a party menu.

- Buy more wine, water and ice than you think you will need.

- Set the table in the morning.

- Get out all the glassware, dishes, serving dishes and cutlery that you will need ahead of time.

- Take a half-hour break from kitchen duties as soon as the first guest arrives, to allow time to greet guests and serve drinks and appetisers.

Hosting an Informal Dinner

Informal dinner parties are a casual way to celebrate a special occasion or simply to get together with friends and family any night of the week. Everything from the mood to the food and drinks should convey a sense of inviting informality. If the weather is good, informal dinners work well outdoors, on a patio or in the garden.

Setting the Table

Giving the occasion a sense of style makes it more enjoyable for your guests, so devote some thought and time to creating a beautiful table, just as you would for a formal dinner party. The basic principles are the same, but fewer pieces are required, and their look and feel can be more varied.

Start with a simple, attractive tablecloth, runner or place mats and add matching or complementary cloth napkins. You can use everyday cutlery, dishes and glasses, or whimsical pieces, such as bamboo plates for an outdoor meal or Asian pottery for an East-West menu. Or mix and match casual pieces with a few formal ones, such as heirloom silver or crystal wineglasses. These festive touches can make all the difference in turning a dinner into a party.

A tumbler or goblet for water and one all-purpose wineglass at each setting are all you need or you can skip the water glass.

Serving the Meal

Welcome guests with drinks and appetisers, served in the living room, kitchen or on the patio. At the table, serve the entire meal family style or begin with a plated first course, set at each place before the guests are seated and then serve the main course and side dishes from platters.

Even at an informal dinner, it is helpful and gracious for the host to serve guests from the head of the table or to make the rounds with the main course on a platter while the guests pass the side dishes. Soups can be ladled from the cooker top or served at the table from a tureen and a salad may be plated or passed in a large bowl.

Serving Dessert

Whether you're hosting a formal dinner party or an informal one, the dessert course is an opportunity to clear the table, change the scene and end on a lively note. If your dessert consists of several elements, it is easiest to plate it in the kitchen. When serving a cake or tart, bring it to the table whole for guests to admire, then serve it from the head of the table or the sideboard.

Plan to serve decaffeinated coffee and tea, but be prepared to offer caffeinated options to guests who want a pick-me-up for the drive home. Have everything set out, and ready to brew before the guests arrive, so you are not scrambling at the last minute.

You might want to serve dessert, a cheese course, coffee and after-dinner drinks in another room. If you do, wait to clear the table and clean up and wash the dishes until after your guests leave. An assortment of small store-bought cookies or candies, such as truffles or mints, served with coffee or after-dinner drinks, makes a nice finish to formal or casual dinners.

INFORMAL SETTING

Start with these basic elements and add or omit pieces depending on your menu.

Napkin Place napkins to the left of each setting or on the centre of each plate.

Bread Plate with Butter Knife Set a small plate above the forks. Place a butter knife across its rim, or pass a spreader.

Forks If serving a salad or first course, put a salad fork in the leftmost position, and the dinner fork just left of the plate.

Dinner and Salad Plates Put a dinner plate at each setting, or bring out with the main course. Use a salad plate for the first or salad course. Or, if serving salad with the main, offer a separate plate.

Knife Set a sturdy table or steak knife, blade inward, to the right of the plate.

Glasses Place a tumbler above the knife for water, and a wineglass to its right. Or you might prefer using just one glass.

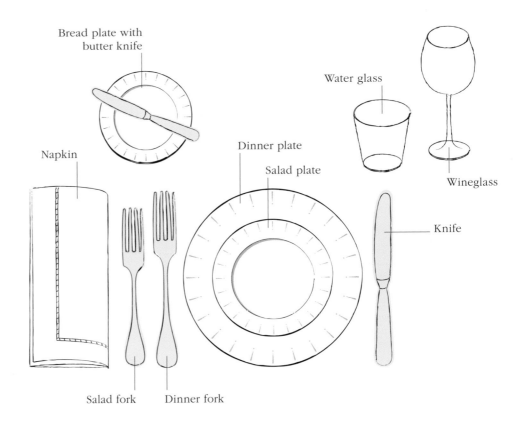

Bread plate with butter knife

Water glass

Napkin

Dinner plate

Salad plate

Wineglass

Knife

Salad fork

Dinner fork

DESSERT SETTING

For both formal and informal dinners, set out dishes and cutlery ahead of time.

Cup and Saucer Place a saucer and cup directly above the dessert setting. For casual dinners, mugs can be used.

Dessert Plate Use small plates for most desserts. Chill plates for cold desserts.

Fork and Spoon Set a dessert fork and teaspoon to the right of the plate. If the dessert calls for a spoon, use a dessert spoon and a teaspoon.

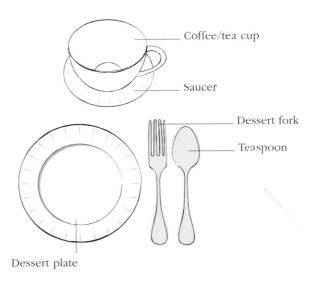

Coffee/tea cup

Saucer

Dessert fork

Teaspoon

Dessert plate

SPRING FAMILY CELEBRATION

HOSTING AND SERVING TIPS

• Set the table in a shady spot; watch the
  path of the light the day before to get a
  sense of where the sun sets.

• Freeze citrus zest, mint leaves or berries in
  water-filled ice-cube trays.

• For an easy hors d'oeuvre, set out goat's
  cheese, strawberries and baguette slices.

• Use a melon baller to scoop out rounds
  of butter; pass at the table with the bread.

• Create informal centrepieces using garden
  flowers in old-fashioned glass jars.

• For wine, serve a dry to fruity white, such
  as Pinot Gris and a light red, such as
  Beaujolais or Pinot Noir.

MENU

Sparkling Mint Lemonade

•

*Baby Spinach Salad with
Parmesan and Papaya*

•

*Roasted Asparagus
with Blood Orange Dipping Sauce*

*Mushroom-Stuffed Chicken
with Spring Vegetables*

•

Strawberry-Rhubarb Galette

WORK PLAN

UP TO 3 WEEKS IN ADVANCE
toast the bread cubes for the stuffing

UP TO 1 DAY IN ADVANCE
make the blood orange dipping sauce
thaw the puff pastry for the galette

UP TO 1 HOUR IN ADVANCE
roast the asparagus

BEFORE DINNER
mix the lemonade
assemble the salad
roast the chicken
bake the galette

gather lemon slices, mint sprigs, citrus (or mint) leaves, a large glass jug, lemongrass stalks (or bamboo skewers, chopsticks or swizzle sticks), crushed ice, cocktail napkins, glasses and a tray.

layer half of the lemon slices in the jug; top with the mint sprigs and then top with another layer of lemon slices, and fill with ice.

thread a lemon slice and a citrus leaf onto the top of each lemongrass stalk. Line the tray with the cocktail napkins. Fill the pitcher with lemonade and place on the tray with the glasses. Put a lemongrass stalk in each glass. Let guests help themselves.

Lemonade for an Outdoor Party

It's easy to make lemonade more special by adding simple creative touches. The more you do to dress up everything, from the jug and the decorations to the glasses and serving tray, the more the drinks become a part of the celebration.

Sparkling Mint Lemonade

Lemonade is a welcome drink when springtime temperatures start to rise. Here, it is mixed in a jug or punch bowl with ice cubes to keep it cold. Serve your guests or let them help themselves.

In a saucepan over medium heat, combine the sugar, water and lemon peel. Bring to the boil, stirring to dissolve the sugar, and boil for 1 minute. Remove from the heat, stir in the 4 mint sprigs, and leave to stand for 30 minutes to infuse the syrup with the mint. Discard the mint sprigs. Strain the syrup through a fine-mesh sieve into a small jug or bowl. Stir in the lemon juice and refrigerate until cold.

Just before serving, transfer the syrup mixture to 1 or 2 jugs or a large punch bowl, add the sparkling water and stir well. Add ice cubes. Serve in tumblers and decorate each serving with a lemon slice and a mint sprig.

Serves 12

500 g (1 lb) granulated sugar

500 ml (16 fl oz) water

4 lemon peel strips, each 7.5 cm (3 in) long, plus 12 lemon slices to decorate

4 large fresh mint sprigs, plus 12 small sprigs to decorate

375 ml (12 fl oz) fresh lemon juice, (8–10 lemons)

3 bottles (1 litre each) sparkling water, chilled

Ice cubes

Baby Spinach Salad with Parmesan and Papaya

Tropical papaya and white balsamic vinegar offer a sweet counterpoint to spinach. Choose papayas that are not too soft or they will be difficult to cut into cubes. Pink peppercorns are milder than black or white and will not compete with the sweetness of the fruit.

Using a vegetable peeler, shave the cheese into thin ribbons. Set aside.

In a large salad bowl, combine the olive oil, vinegars, salt and ground peppercorns and mix well with a fork or whisk. Add the spinach and toss well to coat. Add the papaya and half of the Parmesan, and turn gently to coat. Top with the remaining Parmesan and garnish with more ground peppercorns. Serve at once.

Serves 10–12

125 g (4 oz) Parmesan cheese

4 tablespoons extra-virgin olive oil

1 tablespoon white balsamic vinegar

2 teaspoons red wine vinegar

1/2 teaspoon sea salt

1 1/2 teaspoons freshly ground pink peppercorns, plus extra for garnish

315 g (10 oz) baby spinach

4 ripe papayas, peeled, seeded, and cut into 12-mm (1/2-in) cubes

ROASTED ASPARAGUS WITH BLOOD ORANGE DIPPING SAUCE

Roasting gives the asparagus a slightly nutty, caramelised flavour that pairs well with the citrus dipping sauce. If you cannot find blood oranges, navel or Valencia oranges combined with 1 tablespoon store-bought raspberry juice makes a fine substitute.

About 48 asparagus spears
(1.5 kg /3 lb), tough ends trimmed

1½ tablespoons extra-virgin olive oil

1 teaspoon sea salt

1 teaspoon freshly ground pepper

DIPPING SAUCE

Juice of 2 blood oranges

4 tablespoons mayonnaise

2 tablespoons crème fraîche

2 tablespoons plain skimmed yoghurt

2 tablespoons blood orange–infused
olive oil or extra-virgin olive oil

¼ teaspoon sea salt

Preheat the oven to 200°C (400°F).

Arrange the asparagus spears in a single layer in 2 shallow baking dishes. Drizzle with the olive oil, then sprinkle with the salt and pepper. Turn the spears several times to coat well. Roast, turning several times, until the asparagus tips are lightly golden and the stalks have darkened, 10–15 minutes. Remove from the oven, cover loosely with aluminium foil, and set aside. (The asparagus can be prepared up to 1 hour in advance.)

To make the dipping sauce, in a small bowl, combine the orange juice, mayonnaise, crème fraîche, yoghurt, olive oil and salt and mix well with a fork or whisk. (The sauce can be prepared up to 1 day in advance and refrigerated.)

Transfer the sauce to individual dipping bowls and serve alongside platters of asparagus. Serve at room temperature.

Serves 10–12

Mushroom-Stuffed Chicken with Spring Vegetables

Baby vegetables are more tender and flavoursome. If they aren't available, use larger ones but parboil them before adding them to the roasting pan.

Preheat the oven to 200°C (400°F). Spread the bread cubes on a baking sheet and toast, turning once, until golden brown, about 15 minutes. Set aside. (The bread cubes can be toasted up to 3 weeks in advance and stored in an airtight container.) Reduce the oven temperature to 180°C (350°F). Select a roasting pan just large enough to accommodate the 2 chickens and place a rack in the pan.

Finely chop the chicken giblets and set aside. In a frying pan over medium heat, melt 60 g (2 oz) of the butter. Add half of the mushrooms, the shallots, ¹/₂ teaspoon each of the salt and pepper and the thyme. Cook, stirring, until the mushrooms are tender, 4–5 minutes. Add 125 ml (4 fl oz) of the stock and transfer to a bowl. Stir in the bread cubes, parsley and chopped giblets.

Rub each chicken inside and out with the remaining butter. Season with the remaining ¹/₂ teaspoon each salt and pepper. Pack the cavities snugly with the stuffing and truss the legs with string. Place on the rack and roast for 30 minutes. Remove the chickens from the oven and discard the string. Place the onions, carrots and potatoes around the chickens and turn to coat with the pan juices. Roast until meat thermometer inserted into the thickest part of the thigh, away from the bone, registers 77°C (170°F) and the vegetables are tender, about 1 hour longer. Transfer the vegetables and chickens to 1 or 2 platters and tent with aluminium foil.

Discard all but 2 tablespoons of the juices from the roasting pan, place over medium heat, add the remaining mushrooms and cook just until softened, 2–3 minutes. Using a slotted spoon, transfer the mushrooms to a bowl. Turn off the heat. Add the brandy and 60 ml (2 fl oz) stock, scraping up any browned bits on the pan bottom. Return the heat to medium-high, add the remaining 190 ml (6 fl oz) stock and cook, stirring, until the sauce is reduced and thickened, 1–2 minutes. Stir in the mushrooms, remove from the heat and cover to keep warm.

Remove the stuffing and carve the chickens. To serve, arrange a piece of chicken on each plate, surround with the stuffing and vegetables and top with the sauce.

Serves 10–12

6–8 baguette slices, 2.5 cm (1 in) thick, cut into 2.5-cm (1-in) cubes

2 chickens, about 2 kg (4 lb) each, with giblets

90 g (3 oz) unsalted butter

500 g (1 lb) mixed fresh mushrooms such as chanterelle, porcini, oyster and field, cut into halves or quarters

45 g (1¹/₂ oz) finely chopped shallots

1 teaspoon salt

1 teaspoon freshly ground pepper

2 teaspoons finely chopped fresh thyme

375 ml (12 fl oz) chicken stock

2 tablespoons finely chopped fresh flat-leaf parsley

12–14 spring onions, all but 2.5 cm (1 in) of the green tops cut off, then cut in half lengthways

8–10 young carrots, with green tops

14–16 small potatoes, cut in half

1¹/₂ tablespoons brandy

Fresh rosemary and thyme sprigs for garnish (optional)

Strawberry-Rhubarb Galette

Strawberries and rhubarb are a classic springtime combination. The galette, a rustic tart that shows off the fruit, can be served with a small scoop of ice cream, a dollop of crème fraîche or whipped cream or on its own with just a dusting of icing sugar.

2 sheets frozen puff pastry, each about 30 by 35 cm (12 by 14 ins) and 6 mm (¼ in) thick

10–12 rhubarb stalks, 750 g–1 kg (1½–2 lb) total weight

250 g (8 oz) granulated sugar

1 kg (2 lb) strawberries, hulled and cut into quarters if large or in half if small

Icing sugar for dusting

Thaw the puff pastry sheets in the refrigerator for 24–36 hours, or according to the directions on the package.

Trim the ends of the rhubarb stalks. Using a paring knife, pull away any strings of fibers visible at the tops and discard. Cut the stalks crossways into 12-mm (½-in) pieces. Put in a saucepan with 155 g (5 oz) of the granulated sugar and leave to stand for 30 minutes.

Place the saucepan over medium heat and cook, stirring often, until the rhubarb is tender but not dissolving, 6–8 minutes. The rhubarb will release its juices. If it seems dry, add 2 or 3 teaspoons water. Set aside and let cool.

On a lightly floured work surface, roll out each puff pastry sheet into a 40-cm (16-in) square, making sure there are no breaks or cracks in the pastry. Cut off the corners to make an uneven circle. Place each circle on a baking sheet lined with baking paper.

In a bowl, mix the rhubarb and strawberries together. Evenly divide the rhubarb-strawberry mixture in the centre of each circle, leaving about 5 cm (2 in) around the edge uncovered. Divide the remaining 95 g (3 oz) granulated sugar between the fruit-topped circles, sprinkling it evenly on top. Fold up the uncovered edge, pleating it loosely and covering all but about a 13-cm (5-in) circle of fruit in the centre of the pastry. Place in the freezer and chill for 20 minutes. Meanwhile, preheat the oven to 180°C (350°F).

Remove the baking sheets from the freezer and immediately place in the oven. Bake until the crusts are puffed and golden brown, 20–25 minutes. Remove from the oven and leave to cool for 10 minutes on the pan on a wire rack. Carefully transfer to a cutting board. Using a fine-mesh sieve, sprinkle a light dusting of icing sugar evenly over the top of each galette. Serve warm, cut into wedges.

Serves 10–12

WEEKNIGHT DINNER

WORK PLAN

UP TO 4 HOURS IN ADVANCE

marinate the pork medallions

bake the brownies

UP TO 1 HOUR IN ADVANCE

prepare the sage and mustard sauce

BEFORE DINNER

assemble the rocket salad

prepare the potatoes

finish the pork medallions

HOSTING AND SERVING TIPS

- Keep the palette neutral, adding colour with flowers, napkins and coasters.

- Tuck herb sprigs into napkins tied with a decorative cord. Use the same herb to decorate the table, plates and platters.

- Scatter votives around the table to provide soft, flattering light.

- Wrap warm sliced bread in a linen napkin and serve on a wooden board at the table.

- Put wine and water in clear glass carafes to keep the look light and sparkling.

- For wine, choose medium-bodied red wines such as Pinot Noir and Côtes du Rhône and light white wines such as Pouilly-Fumé and Sauvignon Blanc.

MENU

*Rocket Salad with Pecorino
and Toasted Pine Nuts*

•

Crushed Red Potatoes

*Pork Medallions with Sage
and Mustard Sauce*

•

*Chocolate-Hazelnut Brownies
with Vanilla Ice Cream*

Rocket Salad with Pecorino and Toasted Pine Nuts

If pecorino, a sheep's milk cheese, is unavailable, use Parmesan instead. Young, tender baby rocket leaves are best for this salad. If you can only find larger leaves, trim off the stems.

In a small frying pan over medium heat, toast the pine nuts, shaking the pan gently, until lightly golden, 2–3 minutes. Transfer to a plate and set aside.

In a large salad bowl, combine the olive oil, vinegars, salt and pepper and mix well with a fork or whisk. Add the rocket and toss to coat evenly.

Divide the rocket among individual chilled salad plates. Using a vegetable peeler, shave the cheese into thin ribbons and divide among the salads. Sprinkle with the pine nuts and serve at once.

Serves 4–6

3 tablespoons pine nuts

3 tablespoons extra-virgin olive oil

1 tablespoon balsamic vinegar

1 teaspoon red wine vinegar

1/2 teaspoon *each* sea salt and freshly ground pepper

125–155 g (4–5 oz) rocket

60 g (2 oz) pecorino cheese

Crushed Red Potatoes

Other potato varieties may be substituted. For a little colour and flavour, stir in finely chopped fresh flat-leaf parsley, thyme or rosemary leaves.

Put the potatoes in a large saucepan and add water to cover by 5 cm (2 in). Add 1 teaspoon of the salt and bring to the boil over high heat. Once the water is boiling, reduce the heat to medium, cover and cook until the potatoes are tender when pierced with a fork, 20–25 minutes. Drain well and return the potatoes to the pan.

Add the olive oil and butter. Using a fork or the back of a wooden spoon, crush the potatoes, breaking them into large, fluffy chunks and mixing in the oil and butter. Season to taste with the remaining salt and the pepper. Transfer to a warmed bowl and garnish with the chives. Serve at once.

Serves 4–6

1 kg (2 lb) red-skinned potatoes

1 1/2–2 teaspoons sea salt

1 tablespoon extra-virgin olive oil

2 tablespoons unsalted butter

1/2–1 teaspoon freshly ground pepper

Fresh chives, cut into 2.5-cm (1-in) lengths, for garnish

2 pork tenderloins, about 375 g
(12 oz) each

2 teaspoons salt

1 teaspoon freshly ground pepper

1¹/₂ teaspoons dried sage

250 ml (8 fl oz) double cream

1¹/₂ tablespoons Dijon mustard

1 tablespoon extra-virgin olive oil

3 tablespoons chicken stock

Fresh sage sprigs for garnish

Pork Medallions with Sage and Mustard Sauce

The medallions, or slices, of pork are quick and easy to cook, making them a good choice for a weeknight dinner party. Sage and mustard pair especially well with the mild, sweet pork.

Cut the tenderloins crossways into slices about 12 mm (¹/₂ in) thick. Place the slices in a single layer on a sheet of cling film. In a small bowl, combine the salt, pepper and 1 teaspoon of the dried sage and stir with a fork or whisk. Sprinkle the mixture evenly on both sides of the slices. Leave to stand at room temperature for up to 1 hour, or cover and refrigerate for up to 4 hours.

Meanwhile, in a saucepan, combine the cream, mustard and remaining ¹/₂ teaspoon dried sage. Place over medium-high heat, bring to the boil and stir until the cream is reduced to 125 ml (4 fl oz), about 4 minutes. Set aside. (The sauce can be prepared up to 1 hour in advance.)

In a large frying pan over high heat, warm the olive oil. Working in batches if necessary, add the pork slices and cook until golden brown, about 2 minutes. Reduce the heat to medium and cook for 2–3 minutes longer. Turn and continue to cook until the slices are golden on the second side and nearly opaque throughout, about 4 minutes longer. Transfer to a warmed platter and tent with aluminium foil.

Raise the heat to high and stir in the chicken stock, scraping up any browned bits clinging to the bottom of the pan. Reduce the heat to medium, stir in the cream mixture and continue to stir until the sauce is reduced to about 80 ml (3 fl oz), 2–3 minutes. Pour the sauce over the pork, garnish with the sage sprigs and serve.

Serves 4–6

Chocolate-Hazelnut Brownies with Vanilla Ice Cream

The key to rich brownies is the quantity of cocoa solids in the chocolate. Choose a chocolate with 62 to 75 percent cocoa solids for the best results. You can substitute toasted walnuts for the hazelnuts or omit the nuts altogether.

Preheat the oven to 180°C (350°F). Butter an 20-cm (8-in) square baking pan.

Spread the hazelnuts in a single layer on a baking sheet. Place in the oven and toast, stirring once or twice, until the skins start to darken and wrinkle, 12–15 minutes. Remove from the oven. When the nuts are cool enough to handle, wrap in a kitchen towel and rub vigorously to remove the skins. Some specks of skin will remain. Chop the nuts and set aside. (The hazelnuts can be toasted up to 2 days in advance and stored in an airtight container.)

Place the chocolate in a metal bowl set over, but not touching, barely simmering water in a saucepan. Heat, stirring occasionally, until the chocolate has melted and is smooth, about 2 minutes. Set the bowl aside.

In a large bowl, using an electric mixer on medium speed, beat the butter until fluffy, about 1 minute. Add the sugar and beat until well blended, about 1 minute. Add the eggs and vanilla and beat until well blended, about 1 minute longer. Add 45 g (1$^{1}/_{2}$ oz) of the flour and the salt and beat well. Add the remaining flour, 45 g (1$^{1}/_{2}$ oz) at a time, beating well after each addition. Add the chocolate and beat until well blended and creamy. Stir in the hazelnuts.

Pour the batter into the prepared pan, spreading it evenly. Bake until puffed and a toothpick inserted in the middle comes out clean, 20–25 minutes. Remove from the oven and leave to cool completely in the pan on a wire rack.

To serve, cut into 5-cm (2-in) squares. Place 2 squares on each dessert plate and add a scoop of ice cream.

Makes 16 brownies

125 g (4 oz) hazelnuts

125 g (4 oz) good-quality plain chocolate

125 g (4 oz) unsalted butter, at room temperature

250 g (8 oz) sugar

2 large eggs, beaten

1 teaspoon vanilla essence

125 g (4 oz) plain flour

$^{1}/_{8}$ teaspoon salt

500 ml (16 fl oz) good quality vanilla ice cream

PROVENÇAL FÊTE

MENU

Fried Artichokes with Aioli

•

*Lettuce and Parsley Salad
with Dijon Vinaigrette*

•

Flageolet Beans with Oregano

Ratatouille

*Boneless Leg of Lamb
with Herbes de Provence*

•

*Plum Gratin with
Honey-Lavender Cream*

WORK PLAN

UP TO 1 DAY IN ADVANCE

make the aioli

partially cook the flageolet beans

make the ratatouille

infuse the cream for the gratin

UP TO 6 HOURS IN ADVANCE

prepare the lamb for roasting

UP TO 2 HOURS IN ADVANCE

fry the artichokes

BEFORE DINNER

assemble the salad

roast the lamb

finish the flageolet beans

make the plum gratin

HOSTING AND SERVING TIPS

- For place cards, write names on ribbon and tie around flower clusters.

- Add a small sprig of dried lavender or rosemary to each dish of salt.

- Serve warm baguettes in a basket lined with a pressed linen napkin or tea towel.

- Use stocky candles in hurricane lamps to add a warm glow to the table.

- For wine, decant chilled rosé into carafes or vintage bottles. Switch to Zinfandel or Barolo for the lamb, if desired.

trim sheets of heavy paper using a ruler as a guide to tear the edges decoratively; write out the menu on each sheet in coloured ink.

cut stalks of lavender the same length as the menus; strip the leaves from each stalk. Cut slits in each menu and thread a lavender stem through the paper.

tie a length of decorative ribbon around each lavender stem and place the menus on the table between each place setting.

LAVENDER MENU CARDS

Hand-lettered menus add a sense of style to the setting, give your guests a taste of what's ahead, and make for a pleasant keepsake to take home. If you are pressed for time, print the menu cards on the computer, using a simple, classic font.

FRIED ARTICHOKES WITH AIOLI

The thinly sliced artichokes turn golden and crisp when fried, perfect for eating by hand. If you make the aioli in advance, keep in mind that the flavour intensifies over time.

To make the aioli, put the salt and garlic in a mortar or small bowl. Using a pestle or the back of a wooden spoon, crush together the salt and garlic to make a coarse paste. Transfer the paste to a large bowl. Using a whisk, beat in the egg yolks. Very slowly drizzle in 125 ml (4 fl oz) of the olive oil while continuing to beat until blended and the mixture starts to stiffen. Do not add too much at once or the mixture will not hold together. Once the mixture has begun to stiffen, drizzle in 60–125 ml (2 4 fl oz) of the remaining olive oil while continuing to beat, stopping when the mixture is quite stiff. Transfer to a serving bowl, cover and refrigerate until ready to serve. (The aioli can be made up to 1 day in advance.)

To prepare the artichokes, fill a large bowl halfway with cold water and add the lemon juice. Working with 1 artichoke at a time, break off about 3 layers of the dark green outer leaves until you reach the pale golden yellow inner leaves. If the inner leaves have any purple colouring or are prickly, remove them. Cut off the top quarter of the leaves, and then trim off the stem. Using a knife or mandoline, cut each artichoke lengthwise into slices 6 mm ($^1/_4$ in) thick and immediately drop the slices into the lemon water.

In a frying pan over medium-high heat, warm the olive oil. When the oil is hot, drain the artichoke slices and pat dry. Working in batches, fry the artichoke slices, turning several times, until crisp and golden, 3–4 minutes. Using a slotted spoon, transfer to paper towels to drain. When all the artichokes are fried, sprinkle with the salt. (The artichokes may be fried up to 2 hours in advance, but don't add the salt until just before serving.)

Transfer the artichokes to a platter and garnish with the lemon wedges. Serve at room temperature with the aioli.

Serves 6–8

AIOLI

$^1/_2$ teaspoon sea salt

2 cloves garlic, coarsely chopped

2 large egg yolks

250 ml (8 fl oz) extra-virgin olive oil

ARTICHOKES

3 tablespoons fresh lemon juice

12–16 baby artichokes

60 ml (2 fl oz) extra-virgin olive oil

1 teaspoon sea salt

Lemon wedges for garnish

BUTTER LETTUCE AND PARSLEY SALAD WITH DIJON VINAIGRETTE

The mustard defines the vinaigrette, so choose a good-quality Dijon mustard, preferably made with white wine. Other fresh herbs, such as finely chopped chives, chervil or tarragon, can be added along with the parsley.

Carefully separate the lettuce leaves. Tear only the largest outer leaves into halves and leave the remaining leaves whole.

In a large salad bowl, combine the olive oil, vinegar, mustard, salt and pepper and mix well with a fork. Add the lettuce, chopped parsley and parsley leaves and toss gently to coat. Serve at once.

Serves 6–8

2 heads round lettuce

3¹/₂ tablespoons extra-virgin olive oil

1¹/₂ tablespoons red wine vinegar

2 teaspoons Dijon mustard

¹/₂ teaspoon sea salt

¹/₂ teaspoon freshly ground pepper

15 g (¹/₂ oz) finely chopped fresh flat-leaf parsley, plus
15 g (¹/₂ oz) leaves

FLAGEOLET BEANS WITH OREGANO

Flageolet beans, small and either pale green or white, are a popular dried bean in Provence and are the classic accompaniment to roast lamb. You can substitute small, white navy beans for the flageolets.

Rinse the beans well in a colander, discarding any misshapen beans or stones. In a large saucepan, combine the beans, water, 1 teaspoon of the salt, the bay leaves and the dried oregano and bring to the boil over high heat. Reduce the heat to low, cover, and simmer until the beans are tender to the bite, 1¹/₂–2 hours. (The beans can be partially prepared up to 1 day in advance. Remove them from the heat just before they are tender, about 1–1¹/₂ hours. The next day, add a little more water and cook, covered, for 20–30 minutes over medium heat until tender.)

Using a slotted spoon, transfer the beans to a bowl. Discard the bay leaves. Stir in the remaining ¹/₂ teaspoon salt, the oregano, pepper and olive oil. Serve hot.

Serves 6–8

315 g (10 oz) dried flageolet beans

2.5 litres (4 ¹/₄ pints) water

1¹/₂ teaspoons salt

2 bay leaves

¹/₂ teaspoon dried oregano

1 tablespoon chopped fresh oregano

¹/₂ teaspoon freshly ground pepper

2 tablespoons extra-virgin olive oil or pan drippings from leg of lamb (page 70)

Ratatouille

Ratatouille is the essence of summer in Provence. Juicy, just-picked tomatoes are essential because their juice forms the basis of the zesty sauce and the mildly acidic tang they impart is a hallmark of a good ratatouille. Making the dish ahead of time allows the flavours to blend.

Bring a large saucepan of water to the boil. Using a slotted spoon, dip the tomatoes in the water for 30 seconds, then place in a colander. When the tomatoes are cool enough to handle, slip off the skins with your fingers or a knife. Coarsely chop the tomatoes, reserving the juice. Set aside.

In a large saucepan over medium-high heat, warm the olive oil. Add the onion and sauté until translucent, 3–4 minutes. Add the garlic and sauté for 1 minute. Add the aubergine and sauté until it has absorbed the oil, about 2 minutes. Add the tomatoes, courgette, peppers, thyme, salt and pepper and stir well. Cook uncovered, stirring occasionally, until the aubergine is easily pierced with a fork, the other vegetables are soft, and the tomatoes have been reduced by one-third to one-half, about 45 minutes. Remove from the heat and stir in the basil.

Transfer to a serving bowl. Serve hot or at room temperature. (Ratatouille can be prepared up to 1 day in advance and refrigerated. Bring to room temperature or reheat and then add the chopped basil before serving.)

Serves 6–8

6 very ripe tomatoes, about 1.5 kg (3 lb) total weight

2 tablespoons extra-virgin olive oil

45 g (1½ oz) chopped onion

6 cloves garlic, finely chopped

1 large aubergine, cut into 2.5-cm (1-in) cubes

3 courgettes, cut into slices 12 mm (½ in) thick

2 red peppers, seeded and cut into 2.5-cm (1-in) pieces

2 teaspoons fresh thyme leaves

1 teaspoon salt

1 teaspoon ground pepper

2 teaspoons finely shredded basil

Boneless Leg of Lamb with Herbes de Provence

Generously studded with garlic and rubbed with a blend of dried herbs characteristic of the region, a leg of lamb is often the centrepiece of a Provençal dinner party. If some of your guests prefer well-done meat, roast the lamb until medium. The end slices will be well done, while the inner slices will be less cooked.

1 boneless leg of lamb, 1.75–2 kg (3 1/2–4 lb), trimmed of excess fat

2 tablespoons extra-virgin olive oil

1 1/2 teaspoons sea salt

1 teaspoon freshly ground pepper

3 tablespoons herbes de Provence

5 cloves garlic, cut lengthways into thin slivers

Fresh rosemary sprigs for garnish

Preheat the oven to 200°C (400°F). Select a shallow roasting pan just large enough to accommodate the lamb.

Open up the leg of lamb. In a small bowl, stir together the olive oil, salt, pepper and herbes de Provence. Rub the herb mixture all over the meat. Roll the lamb back to its original shape. Tie at regular intervals with 3 or 4 lengths of kitchen string. Tie another length of string lengthways around the rolled lamb. Using a sharp knife, make 20–25 deep slits in the meat, spacing them regularly. Insert a garlic sliver in each slit. (The lamb can be prepared up to 6 hours in advance and refrigerated. Bring to room temperature before roasting.)

Place the lamb in the pan and roast for 15 minutes. Reduce the oven temperature to 180°C (350°F) and continue to roast until a meat thermometer inserted into the thickest part of the lamb registers 52°C (125°F) for rare, about 30 minutes longer, or 54°–60°C (130°–140°F) for medium, 35–40 minutes longer. Remove from the oven and transfer the lamb to a cutting board. Tent with aluminium foil and let rest for at least 15 minutes. Reserve the pan drippings if using for the flageolet beans (see page 66).

Cut the strings from the lamb and discard. Carefully cut the lamb into slices 12 mm (1/2 in) thick. Arrange on a warmed serving platter, garnish with the rosemary sprigs and serve at once.

Serves 6–8

Plum Gratin with Honey-Lavender Cream

The thickened, lavender-infused cream recalls the flavour of honey-lavender ice cream, a specialty of Provence. The sweetness of the honey and the richness of the cream marry well with the tart plums.

Preheat the oven to 220°C (425°F). Generously butter a 23-cm (9-in) round or oval flameproof dish. Sprinkle 3 tablespoons of the sugar over the bottom.

Cut the plums in half and remove the stones. Cut each half into slices 12 mm (¹/₂ in) thick. Put the slices in the prepared dish, arranging them snugly in a single layer of concentric circles. In a bowl, using a whisk, beat the eggs until lemon yellow, about 30 seconds. Beat in the milk, flour and salt to make a smooth batter. Pour evenly over the plums. Sprinkle with the remaining 90 g (3 oz) sugar and the almonds. Dot with the butter.

Bake the gratin until the batter is puffed and golden, the butter and sugar have formed a crust, and the plums have softened, about 15 minutes. If necessary, place under the grill to finish browning the crust.

Meanwhile, make the honey-lavender cream: In a small saucepan over high heat, combine the cream, honey and lavender and bring to a boil. Cook, stirring, until the cream has reduced by about one-third, about 5 minutes. Remove from the heat and set aside to cool. Strain the cooled cream through a fine-mesh sieve placed over a small bowl. (The cream can be made up to 1 day in advance and refrigerated. Bring to room temperature before serving.)

To serve, spoon the warm gratin into small dessert bowls and drizzle the honey-lavender cream over each serving.

Serves 6–8

125 g (4 oz) sugar

4 or 5 large plums

2 large eggs

125 ml (4 fl oz) whole milk

75 g (2¹/₂ oz) plain flour

¹/₈ teaspoon salt

60 g (2 oz) coarsely chopped almonds

2 tablespoons unsalted butter, cut into small pieces

HONEY-LAVENDER CREAM

160 ml (5 fl oz) double cream

1 tablespoon plus 1 teaspoon lavender or wildflower honey

1 teaspoon pesticide-free fresh or dried lavender blossoms without stems, crushed

ELEGANT DINNER

HOSTING AND SERVING TIPS

- Use a light-coloured linen runner to let the rich wood of the table show.

- Touches of silver add elegance: vases, candlesticks, napkin rings and silver-rimmed plates and serving platters.

- Make small floral centrepieces that pick up the colours of the table setting.

- Use candles in a variety of colours to create a stylish, modern look.

- For an easy hors d'oeuvre, toss mixed olives with strips of citrus zest.

- For wine, serve a Sauvignon Blanc or an off-dry Riesling with the soup and a big Cabernet Sauvignon with the beef.

Grapefruit Martinis

•

*Golden Beet Soup with Crème Fraîche,
Dill and Salmon Roe*

•

*Brussels Sprouts, Pancetta
and Caramelised Onions*

*Black-Pepper Beef Tenderloin
with Celeriac*

•

*Lemon Custards
with Lemon Verbena Cream*

WORK PLAN

UP TO 1 DAY IN ADVANCE

caramelise the onions for the Brussels sprouts

prepare the lemon custards

UP TO 4 HOURS IN ADVANCE

roast the beets for the soup

UP TO 2 HOURS IN ADVANCE

prepare the celeriac

BEFORE DINNER

mix the cocktails

finish the soup

cook the Brussels sprouts

roast the tenderloin

make the lemon verbena cream

Heirloom Napkin Place Cards

Antique silver can dress up any table setting, from modern to traditional. Look for vintage napkin rings at charity shops and car boot sales. Collect a variety of styles; their individual designs are part of their charm. Gather an equal number of matching linen napkins.

gather silver napkin rings, silvered leaves (from a wholesale floral supplier), and card. Cut leaf shapes from the card, and write a guest's name on each leaf with a silver marker.

fold each napkin and thread it through a napkin ring, so that the fabric is cinched in the centre and the ends flair out in an attractive bow tie shape.

attach each name card to a decorative leaf with double-sided tape and slide the end of the leaf under the napkin ring. Place the napkins across the plates.

60 g (2 oz) caster sugar

1 large pink grapefruit wedge, plus 8 segments

Ice cubes

500 ml (16 fl oz) Ruby Red grapefruit vodka

60 ml (2 fl oz) Cointreau

1¹/₂ teaspoons raspberry juice

1 kg (2 lb) golden beets

1 tablespoon extra-virgin olive oil

1 teaspoon salt

1 teaspoon freshly ground pepper

1.25 litres (40 fl oz) chicken stock

125 g (4 oz) crème fraîche

90 g (3 oz) salmon roe

Fresh dill sprigs for garnish

GRAPEFRUIT MARTINIS

Grapefruit vodka, one of the new flavoured vodkas, makes a zesty martini. The Cointreau, replacing the usual vermouth, intensifies the citrus taste.

Select 8 martini glasses. Put the sugar on a small plate. Rub the outside rim of each glass with the large grapefruit wedge. Holding the glass at an angle, roll the outside rim in the sugar. Put the glasses in the freezer to chill for at least 30 minutes.

Fill a cocktail shaker half full with ice and add half each of the vodka, Cointreau and raspberry juice. Cover with the lid and shake for 20 seconds. Strain into 4 of the glasses and add a grapefruit segment to each glass. Repeat to make 4 more martinis. Serve at once.

Serves 8

GOLDEN BEET SOUP WITH CRÈME FRAÎCHE, DILL AND SALMON ROE

Roasting the beets deepens the flavour of the finished soup. For a perfectly smooth soup, pass it through a fine-mesh sieve after puréeing.

Preheat the oven to 180°C (350°F). If the beet greens are attached, cut them off, leaving 2.5 cm (1 in) of the stem intact (reserve the greens for another use). Place the beets in a baking dish and drizzle with the olive oil. Sprinkle with the salt and pepper and spread in a single layer. Roast until tender when pierced with a fork, about 1¹/₂ hours, or longer if the beets are large. Cool, remove and discard the skins and coarsely chop. (The beets can be roasted up to 4 hours in advance.)

In a large saucepan, combine the beets and chicken stock, bring to a boil, reduce the heat to low and simmer until the beets are heated through, 10–15 minutes. Purée the soup until smooth, reheat if necessary, and taste and adjust the seasoning.

Ladle the soup into warmed bowls and top with a dollop of crème fraîche and then a spoonful of salmon roe. Garnish with the dill sprigs and serve.

Serves 6–8

Brussels Sprouts, Pancetta and Caramelised Onions

Pairing roasted Brussels sprouts with caramelised onions brings out the sprouts' natural sweetness, as does the balsamic vinegar. The tangy saltiness of the pancetta balances the flavours.

Cut the onions crossways into very thin slices, using a mandoline if possible, then cut the slices in half and set aside. In a frying pan over medium-high heat, cook the pancetta, stirring occasionally, until it is crisp and has released its fat, 8–10 minutes. Using a slotted spoon, transfer the cooked pancetta to a small plate lined with paper towels to drain and set aside.

Preheat the oven to 230°C (450°F). Add the butter and 1 tablespoon of the olive oil to the fat in the pan. Add the onions, reduce the heat to low and cook uncovered, stirring occasionally, until deep golden brown, about 20 minutes. Remove from the heat and set aside. (The onions can be cooked up to 1 day in advance, covered and refrigerated. When ready to use, reheat with 1 teaspoon olive oil.)

Meanwhile, put the Brussels sprouts in a bowl and add the remaining 1¹/₂ tablespoons olive oil and 1 teaspoon of the balsamic vinegar. Stir well to coat. Sprinkle with the salt and pepper. Transfer the Brussels sprouts to a nonstick baking sheet and spread in a single layer. Roast until tender when pierced with a fork and the edges are lightly browned, about 20 minutes.

Add the roasted Brussels sprouts to the onions along with the reserved pancetta and remaining 1 teaspoon balsamic vinegar. Cook over medium heat, turning to mix well, until the flavours are blended, 4–5 minutes. Transfer to a warmed serving dish and serve at once.

Serves 6–8

250 g (¹/₂ lb) onions

250 g (¹/₂ lb) thinly sliced pancetta, cut into 12-mm (¹/₂-in) pieces

2 tablespoons unsalted butter

2¹/₂ tablespoons extra-virgin olive oil

1 kg (2 lb) Brussels sprouts, halved lengthways

2 teaspoons balsamic vinegar

¹/₂ teaspoon salt

¹/₂ teaspoon freshly ground pepper

BLACK-PEPPER BEEF TENDERLOIN WITH CELERIAC

Horseradish is used to flavour puréed celeriac in a surprise twist on the classic pairing of beef and horseradish. The black-pepper rub makes a fine crust for the tenderloin and marries well with the peppery taste of the horseradish.

Preheat the oven to 230°C (450°F). Place a wire rack in a shallow roasting pan just large enough to accommodate the beef tenderloin. Rub the tenderloin all over with the olive oil, salt and pepper.

Roast until a meat thermometer inserted into the thickest part of the beef registers 46°–49°C (115°–120°F) for rare, about 20 minutes; 52°–54°C (125°–130°F) for medium-rare, about 25 minutes; or 54°–60°C (130°–140°F) for medium, about 30 minutes. Transfer to a cutting board and tent with aluminium foil. Let the tenderloin rest for about 15 minutes.

While the tenderloin is roasting, prepare the celeriac: Using a knife, remove the coarse brown skin. Rinse the celeriac and then cut into 2.5-cm (1-in) cubes. Put the cubes in a large saucepan and add water to cover by 7.5 cm (3 in). Add the salt and bring to the boil over high heat. Reduce the heat to medium and cook until the cubes are tender when pierced with a fork, about 15 minutes. Drain, return to the saucepan, and cover. (This can be done up to 2 hours in advance.)

About 10 minutes before serving the tenderloin, in a small saucepan over medium heat, combine the cream, milk and butter and heat until steaming but not boiling, 2–3 minutes. Pour over the celeriac. Using a potato masher or the back of a fork, mash the celeriac until it forms a coarse purée. Stir in the horseradish, salt and pepper. Taste and adjust the seasoning. Cover and keep warm.

Cut the beef into slices 12 mm (½ in) thick. Spoon the celeriac onto one side of a warmed serving platter and sprinkle with the celeriac leaves. Arrange the beef slices on the other side of the platter and serve at once.

Serves 6–8

1 beef tenderloin, 1.25–1.5 kg (2½–3 lb)

2 tablespoons extra-virgin olive oil

1½ teaspoons sea salt

1 tablespoon freshly ground pepper

CELERY ROOT

1.25 kg (2½ lb) celeriac (about 1 large root)

1 teaspoon sea salt

2 tablespoons double cream

2 tablespoons whole milk

3 tablespoons unsalted butter

2 tablespoons prepared horseradish

1 teaspoon sea salt

1 teaspoon freshly ground pepper

Chopped celery root leaves or celery leaves for garnish

LEMON CUSTARDS WITH LEMON VERBENA CREAM

The bright lemon flavour of fresh verbena leaves infuses the cream used to decorate this classic custard. Look for fresh verbena at speciality stores or farmers' markets.

In the top of a double boiler set over, but not touching, barely simmering water, stir together the cornflour, sugar and salt. Add the boiling water and whisk until well blended, about 3 minutes. Remove the top of the double boiler and cook the cornflour mixture directly over medium-low heat, stirring constantly, until thick and clear, about 5 minutes. Put the egg yolks in a bowl, whisk until blended and then whisk in about 60 ml (2 fl oz) of the cornflour mixture. Pour into the top of the double boiler and continue to cook over medium heat, stirring constantly, until thickened, 2–3 minutes. Remove from the heat and stir in the lemon zest and juice and the butter. Pour into individual ramekins or glasses and leave to cool for at least 2 hours at room temperature. (The custard can be prepared up to 1 day in advance and refrigerated. Bring to room temperature before serving.)

To make the lemon verbena cream, in a small saucepan over medium heat, bring the cream to a simmer. Stir in the sugar and lemon verbena leaves and cook, stirring, until the sugar dissolves, 2–3 minutes. Remove from the heat and leave to stand for 3–4 hours to infuse the cream. Discard the leaves. Return the pan to the hob and bring the cream to the boil over medium-high heat, stirring constantly. Continue to cook until the cream has reduced by half and has thickened, about 5 minutes. Cool to warm or room temperature before serving.

Drizzle the cream over the custard and decorate each serving with a small sprig of lemon verbena. Serve at once.

Serves 6–8

45 g (1^1/2 oz) cornflour

315 g (10 oz) sugar

^{1}/4 teaspoon salt

375 ml (12 fl oz) boiling water

3 large egg yolks

^{1}/2 teaspoon finely grated lemon zest

80 ml (3 fl oz) fresh lemon juice (about 2 lemons)

2 tablespoons unsalted butter

LEMON VERBENA CREAM

250 ml (8 fl oz) double cream

60 g (2 oz) sugar

6–8 fresh lemon verbena leaves

6–8 fresh small lemon verbena sprigs to decorate

SUMMER PATIO PARTY

WORK PLAN

UP TO 2 DAYS IN ADVANCE

make the herb butter

UP TO 1 DAY IN ADVANCE

toast the baguette slices for the bruschetta

UP TO 6 HOURS IN ADVANCE

prepare the orzo

BEFORE DINNER

mix the drinks

make the bruschetta

finish the orzo salad

grill the halibut

grill the peaches

HOSTING AND SERVING TIPS

- For an easy centrepiece, cut large, bright summery flowers, such as zinnias, peonies, daisies and sunflowers, to make a low, domed arrangement in a white bowl. Use floral foam, if needed, to anchor stems.

- Set candles in hurricane lamps for wind-proof illumination as the sun goes down.

- Anchor the tablecloth with old-fashioned wooden clothespeg or weight the corners with stones.

- For wine, serve a citrusy white such as Sauvignon Blanc or Chardonnay; or pour a light red, such as a Beaujolais or Côtes du Rhône.

MENU

Mango-Guava Coolers

Watermelon and Tequila Frescas

•

Gorgonzola Bruschetta with Figs

•

*Orzo Salad with Basil
and Tomatoes*

Grilled Halibut with Herb Butter

•

Grilled Peaches with Toasted Almonds

fold a freshly pressed napkin into a Z by turning one-quarter of the fabric under and one-quarter over, so the edges overlap slightly in the middle.

flip the sides inward to make two flaps, each about one-third of the width of the folded napkin, then fold in half.

pat each napkin flat to set the folds; set each napkin on a plate and tuck a single flower, such as a cosmos or zinnia, in the pocket.

POCKET NAPKIN FOLD

Colourful woven napkins double as a pocket for a delicate summer blossom. For windproof place cards, write guests' names on stones, beach glass, shells or driftwood using a permanent or metallic marker, and place one on each napkin.

Mango-Guava Coolers

In hot summer weather, a combination of fruit juices makes a refreshing aperitif to welcome your guests. This one is decorated with a strawberry to bring out the flavour of the guava juice. A mango cube or two on a cocktail stick would be an equally good choice.

Select 8 tall glasses. Put a few ice cubes in each glass. Pour 60 ml (2 fl oz) of the mango juice, 125 ml (4 fl oz) of the guava juice, 1 tablespoon lime juice, and about 125 ml (4 fl oz) of the sparkling water into each glass and stir. To decorate, balance a strawberry on the rim of each glass. Serve at once.

Serves 8

Ice cubes

500 ml (16 fl oz) mango juice

1 litre (32 fl oz) guava juice

125 ml (4 fl oz) fresh lime juice (3–4 limes)

500 ml (16 fl oz) sparkling water

8 strawberries, slit lengthways nearly in half with stem end intact to decorate

Watermelon and Tequila Frescas

Here, fresh fruit puréed with a little ice and spiked with tequila is a colourful alternative to the usual margarita. The watermelon can be prepared a day in advance and kept covered in the refrigerator.

Select 8 tumblers or old-fashioned glasses. Set aside 8 watermelon cubes for garnish. In a blender, combine half each of the remaining watermelon, the ice, the lime juice and the tequila. Purée until smooth. Pour into 4 of the glasses. Repeat to make 4 more drinks. To decorate, sandwich a reserved watermelon cube between 2 mint leaves on a cocktail stick and balance it on the rim of each glass. Serve at once.

Serves 8

1 small seedless watermelon, about 1.25 kg (2 1/2 lb), flesh removed from rind and cut into 2.5-cm (1-in) cubes

250 g (8 oz) crushed ice

125 ml (4 fl oz) fresh lime juice (3–4 limes)

180 ml (6 fl oz) tequila

16 fresh mint leaves to decorate

Gorgonzola Bruschetta with Figs

Grilled slices of baguette bring out the flavour of the cheese and the figs, an appealing combination of salty and sweet.

20 baguette slices, 6 mm (¹/4 in) thick (about 1 baguette)

2 tablespoons extra-virgin olive oil

250 g (8 oz) Gorgonzola cheese, at room temperature

10–12 ripe, soft figs, coarsely chopped

Fig leaves for garnish, optional

Prepare a charcoal or gas grill for direct grilling over high heat. Lightly oil the grill rack and position it 15 cm (6 in) from the heat source.

Drizzle one side of the baguette slices with the olive oil and place, coated side down, on the grill rack. Grill until lightly golden, 3–4 minutes. Turn and grill until the second side is dry, about 1 minute longer. Remove from the grill. (The baguette slices can be grilled up to 1 day in advance.)

Spread each slice with about 1 tablespoon of the Gorgonzola and top with about 1 tablespoon of the chopped figs. Place fig leaves, if using, on a platter and arrange the bruschetta on top. Serve at once.

Serves 6–8

Orzo Salad with Basil and Tomatoes

Orzo is a good choice for salad because the individual ricelike shapes can be coated thoroughly with the dressing and other seasonings. For extra flavour, add 1 cup stoned, whole Mediterranean-style black olives.

Remove the stems from the tomatoes. Cut large or medium tomatoes into 12-mm ($^1/_2$-in) cubes. Cut the cherry tomatoes in half. Set aside.

Bring a large pot of water to the boil. Add $1^1/_2$ teaspoons of the salt and the orzo. When the water returns to the boil, reduce the heat to medium and cook until the pasta is al dente, about 9 minutes or according to package directions. Drain and place in a large bowl. (The orzo can be prepared up to 6 hours in advance, tossed with a small amount of olive oil to keep it from sticking, and refrigerated. Bring to room temperature before serving.)

Add the tomatoes, remaining $^1/_2$ teaspoon salt, olive oil, vinegar and pepper and turn gently until all the ingredients are well mixed. Add half of the basil and turn again until well mixed. Garnish with the remaining snipped basil and the whole leaves. Serve at room temperature.

Serves 6–8

500 g (1 lb) mixed tomatoes of various sizes, including cherry tomatoes

2 teaspoons salt

655 g (21 oz) orzo pasta

2 tablespoons extra-virgin olive oil

1 teaspoon red wine vinegar

1 teaspoon freshly ground pepper

15 g ($^1/_2$ oz) fresh basil leaves, snipped into small pieces, plus 4–6 whole leaves for garnish

GRILLED HALIBUT WITH HERB BUTTER

HERB BUTTER

125 g (4 oz) unsalted butter,
at room temperature

1 teaspoon freshly chopped fresh chives

1 teaspoon freshly chopped fresh flat-
leaf parsley

1 teaspoon freshly chopped fresh
chervil

6–8 halibut fillets or steaks, each about
185 g (6 oz) and 2.5 cm (1 in) thick

2 tablespoons extra-virgin olive oil

1 teaspoon sea salt

1 teaspoon freshly ground pepper

When a dollop of herb butter is placed on a hot halibut fillet, it melts immediately, infusing the fish with its flavour. Halibut is a very lean fish and cooks quickly, so be careful not to overcook it.

To make the herb butter, cut the butter into slices 2.5 cm (1 in) thick and put in a bowl. Add the chives, parsley and chervil and mash with a fork or the back of a wooden spoon until evenly blended. Pack the butter tightly into a ramekin just large enough to hold it. Cover the ramekin with plastic wrap and refrigerate until ready to serve. (The herb butter can be made up to 2 days in advance; bring to room temperature before serving.)

Prepare a charcoal or gas grill for direct grilling over high heat. Lightly oil the grill rack and position it 15–20 cm (6–8 in) from the heat source. Rub the fillets on both sides with the olive oil and sprinkle with the salt and pepper. Grill until lightly golden and opaque halfway through, about 5 minutes. Turn and grill the fillets until lightly golden on the second side and the flesh easily flakes when tested with a fork, 4–5 minutes longer.

Transfer the fillets to individual plates and top each fillet with a tablespoon of the herb butter. Serve at once.

Serves 6–8

Grilled Peaches
with Toasted Almonds

Grilling brings out the subtle flavour of the peaches, and the halved fruits will heat through quickly. Using a metal brush, clean the grill rack well to make sure no other flavor is imparted to the peaches.

Preheat the oven to 180°C (350°F). Spread the almonds in a single layer on a baking sheet. Place in the oven and toast, stirring once or twice, until fragrant and dark brown, about 15 minutes. Remove from the oven, carefully transfer to a cutting board, and cool. Coarsely chop and set aside. (The almonds can be toasted up to 2 days in advance and stored in an airtight container.)

Prepare a charcoal or gas grill for direct grilling over high heat. Lightly oil the grill rack and position it 15 cm (6 in) from the heat source.

Lightly brush the peach halves all over with the olive oil. Place, round side down, on the grill rack and grill until grill marks appear, about 2 minutes. Using tongs, turn and grill again until grill marks appear on the cut side and the peaches are warmed through, about 4 minutes longer.

Place 2 halves on each plate, spoon on a little cream, and sprinkle with some of the almonds. Serve at once.

Serves 6–8

75 g (2^1/$_2$ oz) almonds

6–8 ripe yellow peaches, halved and stoned

2 teaspoons extra-virgin olive oil

125 ml (4 fl oz) double cream, lightly whipped

HARVEST GATHERING

HOSTING AND SERVING TIPS

- Decorate the table and the space in warm autumn hues of amber, gold, brown, copper and taupe.

- Layer round place mats over rectangular ones to add texture and colour.

- Decorate the mantle or sideboard with fall fruit, such as pomegranates or apples; branches; and votives.

- Fold napkins into squares, tie each with a length of ribbon, and tuck in a spray of dried grass or wheat.

- For wine, choose a light and spicy red, such as Syrah or Pinot Noir. For the white, serve an off-dry Riesling or a citrusy Sauvignon Blanc.

MENU

Spiced Apple Cider

•

*Manchego Cheese and Quince Paste
with Sesame Flatbread*

•

Celery, Pear and Toasted Hazelnut Salad

*Butternut Squash Ravioli
with Brown Butter and Pecans*

•

Apple-Pear Crumble

WORK PLAN

UP TO 1 DAY IN ADVANCE
make the flatbread
prepare the celery for the salad

UP TO 12 HOURS IN ADVANCE
make the ravioli filling

UP TO 2 HOURS IN ADVANCE
make the ravioli

BEFORE DINNER
prepare the cider
assemble the salad
cook the ravioli
make the crumble

Hedgerow Mini Bouquets

Instead of making a single large centrepiece, create a row of matching small ones to run down the centre of the table. This strategy creates a light, airy look and a feel of casual wine-country elegance. It also keeps sight lines clear for conversation.

gather a mix of dried autumn flowers and grasses in shades of gold and green, such as scabiosa, goldenrod, pompom balls, yarrow and hydrangea.

assemble compact bouquets, starting with one type of foliage and adding another variety or two to form a nicely rounded shape and an attractive balance of colour.

wrap each bouquet with several strands of raffia and tie into a rough knot or bow. Splay out the stems to create a flat base. Stand each bouquet upright on a small plate or coaster.

SPICED APPLE CIDER

The crisp, clean taste of naturally fermented apple cider is given a hint of spice with the addition of star anise, clove and cardamom.

Select 8 tumblers or wineglasses. Pour 125 ml (4 fl oz) of the apple cider into each glass. Add $^1/_8$ teaspoon each of the cloves and cardamom to each glass and stir until well blended. Garnish with a star anise. Serve at once.

Serves 8

1 litre (32 fl oz) strong apple cider, chilled

1 teaspoon freshly ground cloves

1 teaspoon ground cardamom

8 whole star anise

MANCHEGO CHEESE AND QUINCE PASTE WITH SESAME FLATBREAD

Membrillo, *or sweet quince paste, is available in well-stocked stores. If pressed for time, use store-bought flatbread.*

In a bowl, stir together the yeast, sugar and warm water. Stand until foamy, about 5 minutes. In another bowl, stir together the flour and rosemary. In a food processor, process the yeast mixture, half of the flour mixture, 1 tablespoon of the olive oil and the salt until mixed, 1–2 minutes. Add the remaining flour mixture and process until a smooth ball forms, about 1 minute. (If the dough seems too dry, add a little water, if it seems too wet, add more flour.) On a lightly floured surface, knead until smooth and elastic, 6–7 minutes, adding the sesame seeds after 5 minutes. Shape the dough into a ball, put in an oiled bowl and turn to coat with the oil. Cover with a damp kitchen towel, put in a warm place and leave to rise until doubled in size, about 1 hour. Punch down, cover and leave to rise again until doubled in size, about 15 minutes.

Position 2 oven racks in the middle of the oven, and preheat to 230°C (450°F). Divide the dough into 3 equal balls. On a lightly floured work surface, roll out each ball into a 30-cm (12-in) round about 6 mm ($^1/_4$ in) thick. Place each round on a baking sheet and brush with the remaining 1 tablespoon olive oil. Place 2 baking sheets in the oven and bake until golden in colour and cooked through, 12–15 minutes. Repeat with the remaining round. Serve hot, warm or at room temperature, broken into pieces. (The flatbread can be baked up to 1 day in advance and stored in an airtight container.) Serve alongside the cheese and quince paste.

Serves 6–8

SESAME FLATBREAD

2 tablespoons active dry yeast

1 teaspoon sugar

375 ml (12 fl oz) warm water, plus 1–3 tablespoons more if needed

515 g (16$^1/_2$ oz) plain flour, plus 1–3 tablespoons more if needed

1$^1/_2$ tablespoons finely chopped fresh rosemary

2 tablespoons extra-virgin olive oil

1 teaspoon salt

60 g (2 oz) sesame seeds

250 g (8 oz) Manchego cheese, cut into thin slices

250 g (8 oz) purchased quince paste, cut into thin slices

8–10 celery sticks

Ice water

75 g (2 1/2 oz) hazelnuts

2 1/2 tablespoons hazelnut oil

1 tablespoon white
balsamic vinegar

1/4 teaspoon salt

1/4 teaspoon freshly ground
white pepper

4 ripe pears, such as Williams, peeled

CELERY, PEAR AND TOASTED HAZELNUT SALAD

Removing the strings from the celery makes thinly slicing the stalks easier and ensures a tender base for this composed seasonal salad. Walnuts and walnut oil can be substituted for the hazelnuts and hazelnut oil.

Preheat the oven to 180°C (350°F).

To remove the strings from the celery, hold each stalk, large end up, and pull the strings downward by trapping them between your fingers and the blade of a paring knife. Using a chef's knife or a mandoline, cut the celery into slices 3 mm (1/8 in) thick. Cut the tops into small pieces. Put all the celery in a bowl of ice water and set aside. (The celery can be prepared up to 1 day in advance and refrigerated.)

Spread the hazelnuts in a single layer on a baking sheet. Place in the oven and toast, stirring once or twice, until the skins start to darken and wrinkle, 12–15 minutes. Remove from the oven. When the nuts are cool enough to handle, wrap in a kitchen towel and rub vigorously to remove the skins. Some specks of skin will remain. Coarsely chop the nuts and set aside.

In a large bowl, combine the hazelnut oil, vinegar, salt and pepper and mix well with a fork. Drain the celery and pat dry with a paper towel. Add to the bowl and turn to coat with the vinaigrette.

Cut each pear in half lengthways. Using a spoon, scoop out the seeds and the fibers surrounding them, as well as the fibres that run down the center from the stem. Cut lengthways into slices 12 mm (1/2 in) thick. Set aside.

Using a slotted spoon, remove the celery from the vinaigrette and divide among chilled salad plates. Arrange the pear slices on top and drizzle with the vinaigrette. Sprinkle with the chopped nuts and serve at once.

Serves 6–8

BUTTERNUT SQUASH RAVIOLI WITH BROWN BUTTER AND PECANS

Squash-filled ravioli is an autumn speciality in Italy. If you have a pasta machine, it will make rolling the dough faster and easier.

Preheat the oven to 190°C (375°F). To make the filling, rub the cut sides of the squash with the olive oil and place, cut side down, on a baking sheet. Bake until tender when pierced with a knife, 1–1^1/$_2$ hours. Let cool, scoop the flesh into a bowl and mash with a fork. Mix in the egg, cheese, salt and spices. Set aside. (The filling can be prepared up to 12 hours in advance and refrigerated.)

In the bowl of a stand mixer fitted with the paddle attachment, whisk together the eggs and salt. With the mixer running on low speed, gradually add 250 g (8 oz) flour, about 45 g (1^1/$_2$ oz) at a time, until most has been added and the dough forms a ball on the paddle. Pinch the dough. It should feel moist but not sticky and be fairly smooth. If not, beat in more flour as necessary. Knead the dough on a lightly floured surface until firm, smooth and moist but not sticky, about 1 minute. Cover with an inverted bowl and rest for at least 30 minutes or up to 2 hours.

Divide the dough in half. On a large, floured surface, roll out one half into a 40-by-50-cm (16-by-20-in) rectangle about 3 mm (^{1}/$_8$ in) thick. Using a knife, lightly mark the dough into 4-cm (1^1/$_2$-in) squares. Place 1 teaspoon filling in the centre of each square. Roll out the remaining dough into a same-sized rectangle and lay it over the filling. Lightly press down on the mounds of filling, then press around each filling to seal. Using a pastry wheel or knife, cut along the length on both sides and across the top and bottom to make 4 cm (1^1/$_2$-in) squares. Crimp the edges to seal. (The ravioli can be made up to 2 hours in advance. Place in a single layer on a floured kitchen towel, dust the tops with flour, and cover with another towel.)

Bring a large pot of water to a boil and add the salt. Working in batches, use a slotted spoon to slide the ravioli into the water. Reduce the heat to low and simmer until tender, 3–5 minutes. Using the spoon, transfer to a warmed platter.

Meanwhile, in a frying pan over medium-high heat, melt the butter. Add the pecans and cook, stirring, until the butter is golden, 2–3 minutes. Cool for about 30 seconds, stir in the lemon juice, and pour over the ravioli. Garnish with the sage.

Serves 6–8

FILLING

1 butternut squash, 1–1.25 kg (2–2^1/$_2$ lb), halved lengthways and seeds discarded

1 teaspoon extra-virgin olive oil

1 large egg, lightly beaten

60 g (2 oz) finely shredded Gruyère cheese

1 teaspoon salt

^{1}/$_2$ teaspoon ground cinnamon

^{1}/$_2$ teaspoon ground cloves

^{1}/$_2$ teaspoon freshly ground pepper

PASTA DOUGH

3 large eggs

^{1}/$_2$ teaspoon salt

315–360 g (10–11^1/$_2$ oz) plain flour

2 teaspoons salt

125 g (4 oz) unsalted butter

30 g (1 oz) coarsely chopped pecans

1 tablespoon fresh lemon juice

1 tablespoon fresh sage leaves for garnish

Apple-Pear Crumble

500 g (1 lb) apples, peeled

500 g (1 lb) pears, peeled

2 teaspoons fresh lemon juice

125 g (4 oz) plain flour

155 g (5 oz) firmly packed
light brown sugar

1/8 teaspoon salt

60 g (2 oz) chilled unsalted butter,
cut into 12-mm (1/2-in) cubes

2 tablespoons pine nuts

Lightly whipped cream for serving

Choose firm apples, such as Granny Smith or Gala, and firm, ripe pears, such as Williams, for the best results. These varieties will soften but still hold their shape when the crumble is baked. The pine nuts in the topping contribute an extra touch of autumn.

Preheat the oven to 190°C (375°F). Butter an 20-cm (8-in) square baking dish.

Halve and core each apple, then cut into 2.5-cm (1-in) cubes. Repeat with the pears. Put all the fruit in the prepared dish. Drizzle with the lemon juice, turning the fruit once or twice to mix well. Spread the fruit evenly in the dish.

In a bowl, stir together the flour, brown sugar and salt. Add the butter and, using a pastry blender or 2 knives, cut the butter into the dry ingredients until the mixture is grainy and the butter pieces are about the size of small peas. Add the pine nuts and mix with a fork or your fingers. Spread the topping evenly over the fruit.

Bake the crumble until the top is golden and the fruit juices are bubbling around the edges, about 50 minutes. Remove from the oven and leave to cool on a wire rack for 10–15 minutes. Serve warm with a dollop of whipped cream.

Serves 6–8

MIDWINTER DINNER

MENU

Cranberry Gin Fizz

•

*Mandarin Orange, Avocado,
Fennel and Olive Salad*

•

Polenta with White Cheddar

Swiss Chard Gratin

Braised Short Ribs

•

*Compote of Dried Fruits
with Clove Biscotti*

HOSTING AND
SERVING TIPS

- Mix pale green foliage or white flowers with holly or bittersweet to create simple table arrangements.

- Use votives or stocky candles on the table and mantle to set a wintry mood.

- For an easy appetiser, toss almonds with fresh rosemary leaves.

- Serve slices of crusty bread, such as *ciabatta,* in a basket lined with a napkin that matches the table setting.

- If you have a fireplace, build a fire and consider serving drinks and appetisers or dessert and coffee beside the hearth.

- For wine, offer a fruity Chardonnay or sparkling wine with the salad; serve Merlot or Syrah with the short ribs.

WORK PLAN

UP TO 5 DAYS IN ADVANCE
bake the biscotti

UP TO 2 DAYS IN ADVANCE
make the compote

UP TO I DAY IN ADVANCE
braise the ribs

UP TO 6 HOURS IN ADVANCE
prepare the chard

BEFORE DINNER
mix the cocktails
assemble the salad
cook the polenta
finish the gratin

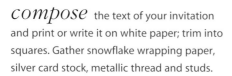

compose the text of your invitation and print or write it on white paper; trim into squares. Gather snowflake wrapping paper, silver card stock, metallic thread and studs.

fold the card in half to make square cards. Use double-sided tape or a glue stick to attach the invitation text inside each folded card. Cut a shape from the decorative paper.

attach the cutout shape using a stud, glue or double-sided tape. Tie a length of metallic or coloured thread around the stud, making an attractive bow.

HANDMADE INVITATIONS

A special invitation sets the tone for a party the moment it is received. Here, the snowflake motif on the vases inspired the look of these sparkling, easy-to-make invitations. Carry the theme through by cutting bands of the same decorative paper to make festive napkin rings.

CRANBERRY GIN FIZZ

A dash of tart cranberry juice gives the gin fizz a colourful winter update. If fresh cranberries are in season, add a few to each drink to decorate.

Select 8 small glasses and put 2 or 3 ice cubes in each glass. Fill a cocktail shaker half full with ice and add half each of the lemon juice, gin, sugar and cranberry juice. Cover with the lid and shake for 20 seconds. Strain into 4 of the glasses. Add 2 tablespoons tonic water to each glass, stir and decorate with the lemon slices. Repeat to make 4 more drinks. Serve at once.

Serves 8

16–24 ice cubes

125 ml (4 fl oz) fresh
lemon juice (3–4 lemons)

500 ml (16 fl oz) gin

2^1/$_2$ tablespoons caster sugar

250 ml (8 fl oz) unsweetened
cranberry juice

125 ml (4 fl oz) tonic water

Lemon slices for garnish

MANDARIN ORANGE, AVOCADO, FENNEL AND OLIVE SALAD

Winter is citrus season, the time to showcase sweet, juicy oranges in a salad with crisp, anise-flavoured fennel and silky, rich avocado.

Cut off the stems and feathery leaves from each fennel bulb. Reserve a few of the leaves for garnish. Trim the base. Discard the outer layer of the bulb if it is tough. Finely slice the bulb crossways into thin pieces. Stone and peel the avocados and cut lengthways into slices 12 mm (^{1}/$_2$ in) thick. Zest each orange until you have 2 teaspoons of zest, then peel each orange and separate the sections, removing any bitter white pith and seeds. Cut the sections in half.

In a salad bowl, combine the olive oil, the orange zest and juice, 1 tablespoon of the balsamic vinegar, the Champagne vinegar, the salt and the pepper and mix well with a fork. Add the fennel, oranges, avocado and olives and toss gently to coat. Divide among chilled salad plates. Drizzle each salad with a little of the remaining 1 tablespoon balsamic vinegar. Garnish with the reserved fennel leaves and serve.

Serves 6–8

2 fennel bulbs

3 avocados

4 mandarin oranges

3 tablespoons orange-infused olive oil
or extra-virgin olive oil

1 tablespoon freshly squeezed
mandarin orange juice

2 tablespoons white balsamic vinegar

1 teaspoon Champagne vinegar

^{1}/$_2$ teaspoon sea salt

^{1}/$_2$ teaspoon freshly ground pepper

75 g (2^1/$_2$ oz) stoned, Mediterranean-
style black olives

Polenta with White Cheddar

You can use any full-flavoured or aged white Cheddar cheese for the polenta; Parmesan makes a good substitute.

Put the water in a large saucepan and add 1½ teaspoons of the salt. Bring to the boil over high heat. Add the polenta in a slow, steady stream, stirring constantly. Reduce the heat to low and cook, stirring frequently, until the polenta pulls away from the sides of the pan, 40–45 minutes.

Stir in the butter, all but 30 g (1 oz) of the cheese, the remaining 1 teaspoon salt and the pepper and cook until the butter and cheese have melted into the polenta, 3–4 minutes longer.

Spoon the polenta into a large warmed bowl and sprinkle with the remaining cheese and some pepper. Serve at once.

2 litres (3¼ pints) water

2½ teaspoons salt

330 g (10½ oz) polenta

3 tablespoons unsalted butter

220 g (7 oz) finely shredded white Cheddar cheese

1 teaspoon freshly ground pepper, plus pepper for sprinkling

Swiss Chard Gratin

Red, green or rainbow chard may be used. Red has a slightly more assertive flavour than green, while rainbow chard is the mildest.

Position a rack 15 cm (6 in) from the heat source and preheat the grill. Oil a flameproof baking dish about 30 cm (12 in) round or square in diameter and 4 cm (1½ in) deep.

In a large saucepan, combine the chard, 1 teaspoon of the salt and water to cover by 10 cm (4 in). Bring to the boil over high heat, reduce the heat to medium and cook until the stems are tender, 15–20 minutes. Remove from the heat, rinse under cold water, squeeze dry and chop coarsely. (The chard can be prepared up to 6 hours in advance.)

In a large frying pan over medium heat, warm the olive oil. Add the garlic, chard, remaining ½ teaspoon salt and the pepper and stir to coat the chard. Transfer to the prepared dish and sprinkle with the cheeses. Grill until the cheeses form a golden brown crust, about 5 minutes. Serve hot.

Each recipe serves 6–8

16 large Swiss chard leaves (about 2 bunches), tough stems trimmed

1½ teaspoons salt

2 tablespoons extra-virgin olive oil

1 clove garlic, finely chopped

¼ teaspoon freshly ground pepper

30 g (1 oz) finely shredded Gruyère cheese

30 g (1 oz) freshly grated Parmesan cheese

BRAISED SHORT RIBS

Bone-in short ribs are delicious when cooked slowly in the oven. If short ribs are unavailable, ask the butcher to cut down full-sized ribs. The flavour of the dish intensifies if cooked a day ahead and reheated.

2.25 kg (4 1/2 lb) bone-in beef short ribs

4 teaspoons salt

4 teaspoons freshly ground pepper

1 tablespoon fresh thyme leaves plus 5 or 6 sprigs and extra leaves for garnish

1 tablespoon paprika

3 tablespoons extra-virgin olive oil

1 onion, chopped

2 carrots, peeled and sliced on the diagonal

3 cloves garlic, chopped

1 tablespoon plain flour

375 ml (12 fl oz) dry red wine such as Syrah or Merlot

375 ml (12 fl oz) water

500 ml (16 fl oz) beef stock

1 1/2 tablespoons tomato purée

2 teaspoons balsamic vinegar

1 bay leaf

Put the ribs in a large bowl. In a cup, mix together 2 teaspoons each of the salt and pepper, the 1 tablespoon thyme leaves and the paprika. Rub the seasonings all over the ribs. Cover and stand for 2–4 hours (refrigerate if longer than 2 hours).

Preheat the oven to 165°C (325°F). In a large heavy based frying pan over medium-high heat, warm the olive oil. Working in batches to avoid crowding, add the ribs in a single layer and cook, turning as needed, until browned on all sides and on the ends, about 5 minutes for each batch. Transfer to a bowl and set aside.

Pour off all but 2 tablespoons of the fat in the pot and return to medium-high heat. Stir in the onion and carrots and cook, stirring often, until the onions have softened, about 2 minutes. Stir in the garlic, then sprinkle the vegetables with the flour. Continue to cook, stirring, until the flour is lightly browned, about 2 minutes. Pour in the wine, scraping up any browned bits clinging to the bottom of the pot. Continue to stir, adding the water, beef stock, tomato purée, vinegar, bay leaf, thyme sprigs and the remaining 2 teaspoons each salt and pepper. Return the ribs and any collected juices to the pot and spoon the liquid over the ribs.

Cover, place in the oven and cook for 1 hour. Uncover, stir the meat, re-cover and continue to cook until the meat has nearly fallen off the bone and can easily be cut with a dinner fork and knife, 2–2 1/2 hours. Remove from the oven and skim off and discard the fat from the surface. (The ribs can be braised up to 1 day in advance. Remove from the heat, cool, cover the pot and refrigerate. The next day, remove from the refrigerator, lift off and discard any fat that has solidified on the surface, and reheat on the cooker top over low heat for 30 minutes, stirring occasionally.)

Transfer to a deep platter, discarding the thyme sprigs and bay leaf. Garnish with the remaining fresh thyme leaves and serve at once.

Serves 6–8

COMPOTE OF DRIED FRUITS WITH CLOVE BISCOTTI

The clove biscotti complement the sweet-tart poached fruits and can be dipped in the compote to soak up the tasty juices. If you want to serve purchased cookies, look for almond biscotti, which will be a nice match with the fruits. Serve the compote with freshly whipped cream, if desired.

To make the biscotti, preheat the oven to 180°C (350°F). Butter a baking sheet and dust with flour. In a large bowl, whisk together the flour, salt, chopped and ground walnuts, bicarbonate of soda and ground cloves. Make a well in the centre and add the eggs, sugar and clove extract. Using an electric mixer or a whisk, beat the eggs and sugar into the dry ingredients until a stiff, sticky dough forms. (If the dough remains too wet, add more flour.) With lightly floured hands, gather the dough into a ball, place on a lightly floured work surface and knead until firm, 2–3 minutes. Divide the dough into 2 or 3 equal portions. Using your palms, roll each portion into a log 4–5 cm ($1^{1}/_{2}$–2 in) in diameter.

Place the logs on the prepared baking sheet, spacing them well apart. Bake until each log is light brown, about 25 minutes. Remove from the oven and cool on the baking sheet for 10 minutes. Using a sharp knife, cut each log crossways on the diagonal into 20–25 slices about 12 mm ($^{1}/_{2}$ in) thick. Place the slices, cut side down, on the baking sheet, spacing them 12 mm ($^{1}/_{2}$ in) apart (you will probably have to bake in batches). Bake until lightly golden on the underside, 7–8 minutes. Remove from the oven, turn the biscotti, and continue baking until faintly golden on the second side, 7–8 minutes longer. Remove from the oven and transfer the biscotti to wire racks to cool. (The biscotti can be made up to 5 days in advance and stored in an airtight container.)

To make the compote, in a saucepan, combine the pears, figs, cherries, wine, water, sugar and star anise and bring to the boil over medium-high heat. Reduce the heat to low and simmer, uncovered, until the fruits are plump, 10–15 minutes. Remove from the heat and stand for at least 30 minutes before serving. (The compote can be made up to 2 days in advance, covered and refrigerated. Warm over low heat before serving.) Remove the star anise or keep for a garnish.

Serve the compote warm in individual bowls. Accompany with the biscotti.

Serves 6–8

BISCOTTI

235 g ($7^{1}/_{2}$ oz) plain flour, plus 1–3 tablespoons more if needed

$^{1}/_{4}$ teaspoon salt

30 g (1 oz) coarsely chopped walnuts

185 g (6 oz) finely ground walnuts

1 teaspoon bicarbonate of soda

$^{1}/_{2}$ teaspoon freshly ground cloves

3 large eggs

125 g (4 oz) sugar

$^{1}/_{2}$ teaspoon clove essence

COMPOTE

10 dried pear halves, cut in half lengthways

16 dried figs, cut in half lengthways

25 dried cherries

250 ml (8 fl oz) sweet white wine such as muscat, Beaumes-de-Venise, or late-harvest Riesling

250 ml (8 fl oz) water

1 tablespoon sugar

1 whole star anise

INDEX

ACKNOWLEDGEMENTS

WELDON OWEN wishes to thank the following individuals for their kind assistance: Birdman Inc., Carla Bourque, Carrie Bradley, Peter Cieply, Diana Coopersmith, Scott Cox, Ben Davidson, Ken Della Penta, Christina Donley, Judith Dunham, Leah Firth, Karen Greenberg, Richard and Judy Guggenhime, Jenny Koehler, Beth Kring, Leilani Marie Labong, Monica Lee, Belinda Levensohn, Mill Nash, Lesli Neilson, Julia Nelson, Danielle Parker, Emily Polar, Eloise Shaw, Georgia Shaw, Sharon Silva, Kara Van Niekerk, Cynthia Wright and David Easton, and Kimberly Wright-Violich and Bill Scott.

GEORGEANNE BRENNAN would like to thank her husband, Jim Schrupp, and all the family and friends who so gleefully participated in recipe tastings around her dinner party table.

LAUREN HUNTER would like to thank the entire creative team at Weldon Owen, her assistant Daniele for all of her hard work helping things flow smoothly on set, and Joe Keller for his thoughtful and beautiful photography, the following manufacturers: Corinth Platinum dinnerware by The Royal China & Porcelain Companies; Cucina Fresca dinnerware by Vietri; Kona Indigo and Colorwave Sky dinnerware by Noritake, and the following San Francisco Bay Area stores: Bac, Columbine, Culinaire, Dandelion, Ellington & French, Heath Ceramics, I Leoni, Lime Stone, Period George, Strawberry Creek, Sue Fisher King, The Gardener, and Trove.

PHOTO CREDITS

KELLER & KELLER, all photography except for the following:

NOEL BARNHURST: Page 100

ANNA WILLIAMS: Page 12

FOOD STYLING CREDITS

ALISON ATTENBOROUGH, all food styling except for the following:

JAMIE KIMM: Spring Family Celebration (pages 26–41) and Summer Patio Party (pages 90–107)

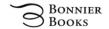

BONNIER BOOKS

Appledram Farms

Birdham Road

Chichester

PO20 7EQ

BONNIER BOOKS WEBSITE

www.bonnierbooks.co.uk

A WELDON OWEN PRODUCTION

Copyright © 2006 Weldon Owen Inc.
and Williams-Sonoma, Inc.

All rights reserved, including the right of
reproduction in whole or in part in any form.

First published in UK by Bonnier Books, 2007

Printed in China

Printed by Midas Printing Limited

ISBN-13: 978-1-905825-37-0

Jacket Images

Back cover: Flageolet Beans with Oregano, page 66;
Ratatouille, page 69; Boneless Leg of Lamb with Herbes
de Provence, page 70; Cranberry Gin Fizz, page 132

THE ENTERTAINING SERIES

Conceived and produced by Weldon Owen Inc.

814 Montgomery Street, San Francisco, CA 94133

Telephone: 415 291 0100 Fax: 415 291 8841

In Collaboration with Williams-Sonoma, Inc.
3250 Van Ness Avenue, San Francisco, CA 94109

WELDON OWEN INC.

Chief Executive Officer: John Owen

President and Chief Operating Officer: Terry Newell

Chief Financial Officer: Christine E. Munson

Vice President, International Sales: Stuart Laurence

Vice President and Creative Director: Gaye Allen

Vice President and Publisher: Hannah Rahill

Associate Publisher: Amy Marr

Senior Art Director: Emma Boys

Associate Editor: Donita Boles

Designer: Anna Migirova

Photo Manager: Meghan Hildebrand

Production Director: Chris Hemesath

Colour Manager: Teri Bell

Co-edition and Reprint Coordinator: Todd Rechner

Assistant Food Stylist: Lillian Kang

Photographer's Assistant: Michael Bennett

Assistant Prop Stylist: Daniele Maxwell